The Power of Print

print marketing in a digital world

DANIEL R. EDWARDS

The Power of Print: print marketing in a digital world
© Daniel R. Edwards 2021

ISBN: 978-1-922644-99-2 (paperback)
          978-1-922644-98-5 (eBook)

 A catalogue record for this
book is available from the
National Library of Australia

Published by Daniel R Edwards and Ocean Reeve Publishing
www.posterboyprinting.com.au
www.oceanreevepublishing.com

Contents

Introduction

You are reading this book because you are a marketer who wants to make the most out of the print medium. You want to learn about how to use print to get the most out of your marketing spend.

I have identified 6 principles, common in great print executions, that can be applied to any print job. The application of just one or two of these principles will increase the return on investment (ROI), whether the print is on its own or an element within a multichannel campaign mix.

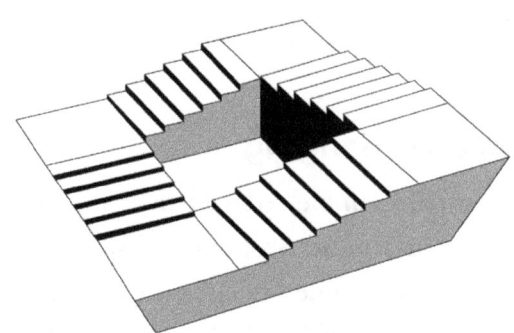

Figure 1: Searching for information on the internet can be likened to the 'Penrose stairs' (the impossible stairs)

You've probably looked around online to learn about print but haven't found much. That's because the internet is often a closed loop. For example, a blogger reads something questionable on Wikipedia and writes an article about it. Wikipedia then references that blog to strengthen its questionable claim. It's a Penrose Stairs of information.

This exact thing has happened to information about marketing. The internet is dominated by digital marketers who write about digital marketing and reference other articles about digital marketing. Suddenly no one in marketing is talking about print or any other traditional marketing and if they are, they're talking about imminent demise of the traditional channels.

TV is dead. Radio is dead. Newspapers are dead. Billboards are dead. Cinema is dead.

Print is dead.

Except, it's not. None of them are.

But, repeated often enough, questionable facts become accepted fact.

In contrast, it is the internet that is starting to soften. The value of the once mighty click is under serious question.

The winds are changing

In 2018, Procter & Gamble reduced their digital ad spend by US$200 million, or around 8%, and it had no effect on their turnover. They have continued to cut the expenditure since.

In 2017, Uber shut off US$150 million (60%) of their programmatic marketing and it had no effect on turnover.

The marketers at eBay were told they were earning $12.28 for every dollar they spent on buying the word 'eBay'. A price dispute led them to shut off keyword advertising for a month. It had no effect on turnover. They began to experiment with cutting more paid word searches. They found that for every dollar they had been spending on keyword advertising, they were losing $0.63 .

JPMorgan Chase cut advertising from 400,000 sites down to 5000 sites and, again, there was no difference.

Fraud

How could major companies make such extensive changes to their marketing spend and suffer massive drops in click-through rates (CTR), yet show no effect on sales?

The answer is simple – the internet is rife with fraud and the victims are marketing budgets.

What does 'internet fraud' mean? Dr Augustine Fou, an expert on internet fraud, defines it well:

Ad fraud in digital marketing is simply ads being shown to bots (software programs) instead of to humans. When marketers buy digital ads, they think the ads are being shown on websites to humans. Marketers are not getting what they paid for, and there will be no business outcomes from these marketing activities.

In 2018, the New York Times published an in-depth investigation[1] on fraud in Twitter. It was discovered that an industry that creates and sells fake, but active, Twitter bot accounts has developed. People buy the bots to boost their own account stats. For some of the real people who bought the 'bot followers', 75% of their million followers were bots. These people were then being paid by marketers to promote products because they were 'influencers'.

The click economy is 'fool's gold'. How much value can be put into a click when there is no way to guarantee it was generated by a person?

But I'm different

How did this happen? How did a whole industry embrace a new marketing format that doesn't work that well? This has happened because marketers tend to be the kind of people who love the internet and they assume everyone else is like them.

Thinkbox, a UK TV trade organisation, did a study[2] comparing marketers' assumptions about the viewing habits of consumers with actual figures. They asked marketers to estimate how many minutes a day a normal person watches YouTube. Respondents said 62 minutes; the actual figure was 16 minutes. Marketers were just as wrong about broadcast TV and subscription TV.

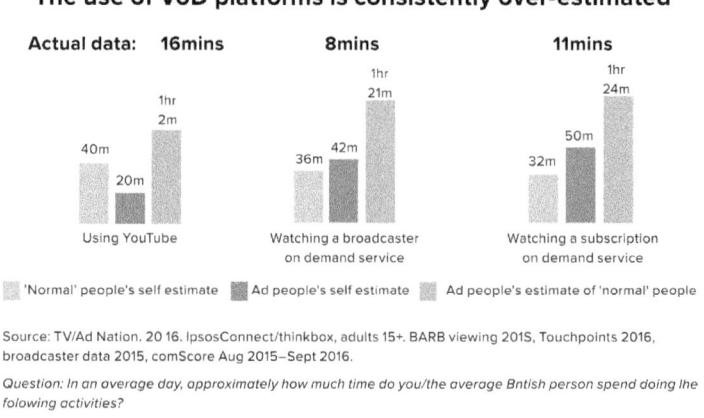

The use of VoD platforms is consistently over-estimated

Source: TV/Ad Nation. 20 16. IpsosConnect/thinkbox, adults 15+. BARB viewing 201S, Touchpoints 2016, broadcaster data 2015, comScore Aug 2015–Sept 2016.

Question: In an average day, approximately how much time do you/the average British person spend doing the following activities?

Figure 2: Marketers' responses when asked how long people spent viewing different platforms

The market is not the marketer.

The same study investigated online platform engagement[3], comparing marketers to normal people. This is like comparing apples and bananas. Marketers are not like most people – they live in a bubble and are much more engaged with online platforms, so are biased towards those channels.

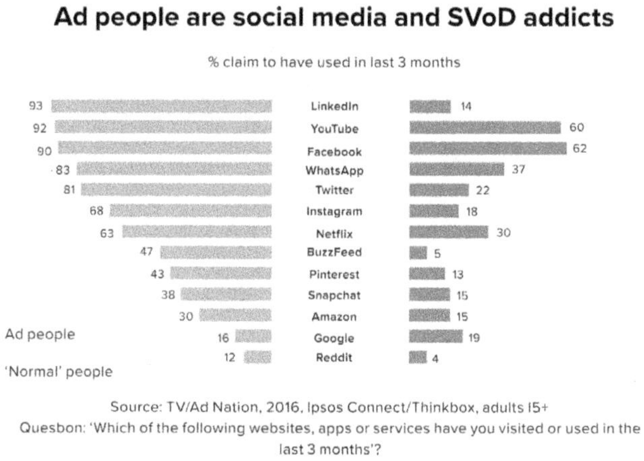

Ad people are social media and SVoD addicts

% claim to have used in last 3 months

Ad people	Platform	'Normal' people
93	LinkedIn	14
92	YouTube	60
90	Facebook	62
83	WhatsApp	37
81	Twitter	22
68	Instagram	18
63	Netflix	30
47	BuzzFeed	5
43	Pinterest	13
38	Snapchat	15
30	Amazon	15
16	Google	19
12	Reddit	4

Source: TV/Ad Nation, 2016, Ipsos Connect/Thinkbox, adults 15+
Quesbon: 'Which of the following websites, apps or services have you visited or used in the last 3 months'?

Figure 3: Engagement with different online platforms, comparing marketers with 'normal' people

Market research company, Ebiquity, published a study[3] in 2020 for UK radio advertising industry group, Radiocentre, which looked at the actual effectiveness of different media platforms compared to the advertising industry's perception of their effectiveness. They asked a representative sample of marketers what they thought the most effective marketing platforms were. This was then compared to the actual platform performance of 100 recent campaigns.

They found that digital marketing was highly valued by advertisers but underperformed in the field. Conversely, print marketing was considered weak by marketers but performed well in the field.

Overall performance ranking

	2020 — Evidence			2020 — perception	
1	TV	108.5	1	TV	52.5
2	Radio	102.5	2	Online video	47.0
3	Newspapers	82.1	3	Radio	46.0
4	Magazines	76.5	4	Social media	44.6
5	Out of home	71.2	5	Out of home	43.1
6	Direct mail	69.6	6	Cinema	42.8
7	Social media	65.0	7	Online display	37.6
8	Cinema	61.4	8	Newspapers	37.5
9	Online video	55.0	9	Magazines	33.6
10	Online Display	49.7	10	Direct mail	33.6

Evidence based on sum of scores for 12 attributes with importance weights applied.

Perception based on sum of mean scores for all 12 attributes with importance weights applied. Base n=102 (each respondent noted 2 attributes)

Figure 4: Actual effectiveness of marketing campaigns versus effectiveness as perceived by marketers

These results mirror those of a similar study[5] done in Australia in 2013 for Australia Post.

Marketers may have fallen in love with exciting new digital toys but the rest of the market hasn't.

Super Coffee

Super Coffee was founded in 2016 by three brothers and, in five years, grew to be valued at US$400 million. In an interview about Facebook strategies for entering a new market[4], CEO of Super Coffee, Jimmy DeCicco, said:

I went there right away. I was like, let's do this. This is brilliant, you know what – we'll geo fence an area that will drive everybody there exactly. Unfortunately, it's a very expensive way to lose money fast because there's zero attribution. We tried it in select markets with select stores, and there wasn't even a meaningful lift in sales, we were just burning cash.

Digital marketing doesn't work on the average consumer.

DeCicco went on:

But what we do as a tactic sometimes is like, if we're, let's say we have a big presentation coming up to get into a grocery chain, we will geo fence the headquarters of that chain so that everybody who's in there just sees our ads.

DeCicco's reflection speaks to this point – digital advertising works on the marketing team in head offices because marketers love digital marketing.

Despite the rapid growth of Super Coffee, they have not changed the tactic they used when they got into their first whole foods outlet. DeCicco adds, 'There's no substitute for a human being going into a store and building a display for samples and educating customers ... even now, on weekends, I go and pour samples because that's what works.'

Part of the Super Coffee marketing approach has been to engage social media influencers. Rather than pay for their services, Super Coffee allows influencers to invest in the company and become owners, with measurable deliverables. Essentially, the influencers become commission-only sales reps. If they promote the product, and there is a measurable impact on sales, they get paid.

Mega celebrities like Jennifer Lopez – she's got 150 million followers on Instagram – she posted herself drinking Super Coffee a few weeks ago and we didn't see it. It wasn't even a blip on the radar ... the nice thing about having J. Lo as an investor is that she could have charged us half a million dollars for that post and it would have been the biggest waste of money we've ever spent.

When asked how he thinks influencers work, DeCicco said, 'I think influencers influence other influencers.'

In the same way that Facebook advertising works on marketers, influencers only work on influencers. Super Coffee acknowledges there is need for general brand awareness to be present on social media but they approach it in such a way it makes them money rather than costing them money.

Super Coffee is a modern company that has been a huge success. Their massive growth is built on a foundation of print, instore visual merchandising and sample displays – all strategies that are decades old. This flies in the face of everything digital marketers tell us. This flies in the face of everything digital marketers tell us. Facebook targeting doesn't work; influencers don't work. It took us a million years to evolve to be the way we are – this is not going to change quickly and Super Coffee proves that.

Marketing, not digital marketing

It is time to drop digital marketing and start marketing. Chief Marketing Officer (CMO) of L'Oréal, Stephan Berube, said:

> *I always smile when agencies claim they are going digital. Honestly, maybe that was good in 2010, but in 2017 they should claim they just do marketing. We need to stop talking about digital – it's all part of marketing*[7.]

Marketing thought leader, Mark Ritson says:

> *Why would you be a digital marketer and restrict yourself to a silo where only half of the tools are relevant to you? Why would you tie one hand behind your back?*

Many large businesses are already using print in their marketing mix. Domino's Pizza and Menulog regularly use letterbox marketing. Coles, Aldi and Woolworths all publish catalogues and magazines.

Even Amazon, the king of digital marketing, is using printed catalogues in the USA.

Don't get me wrong – internet marketing is a powerful and critical tool for any business but it has its limits. A good marketing campaign will integrate across multiple communication channels and, today, one of them is absolutely the internet. Another one should be print.

One of the more successful real estate agents I know, Shannon, is also the most rounded marketer I know. He uses drones to get amazing photography of his properties and creates short videos about each one. He invests in the dominant websites to post his videos and photographs. While setting up his open homes, he drops off 200 flyers advertising for new houses to sell, 50 each side and 100 across the road. He puts up a big sign at the front of the house. During the open home, he gets visitors to tap their details into an iPad that feeds into his CRM, and he hands out brochures and business cards. Shannon elegantly uses every marketing tool at his disposal to market his business and he sells more houses than any other agent in his area.

Print design

I have worked in print for almost 20 years to date. What most people get wrong is they don't see print as anything more than a vehicle to carry the ink with their message on it. It's a broken iPad that just shows a single image. To really get the most out of print, you need to embrace the fact it is a real thing in the real world.

This book grew from the years I have spent in the print industry – working on graphic design, getting ink on my hands and toner up my nose, climbing ladders, riding cherry-pickers, and visiting shopping centres in the middle of the night to install printed images. I've worked with hundreds of Australia's top marketers on many thousands of print projects.

I've had hands-on experience as print production has evolved from a mechanical process, using decades-old machines, to rapid yearly technical advances – each printing marvel quickly over-shadowed by the next. The technological advances have been enormous. Today, there are things possible in print that were not possible only two years ago.

I have been on the frontline as evolving print technology changed the print industry and the internet changed the world.

I have studied many of the best print campaigns from around the world and identified the factors that made each one effective. I call these the principles of print design and outline them in the 6 chapters of this book. If you can apply just one or two of these principles to any print collateral, the object you produce will be an exciting and remarkable element of a marketing campaign.

Future you

By the time you have finished this book, you will have the tools to develop remarkable printed pieces that will provide solid value and ROI from the medium beyond that which has already been realised through graphic design and calls to action.

My hope is that as you stop thinking about print as a broken iPad and start treating it as a crucial aspect of your marketing mix and sales drive, you will begin to see what a dynamic and exciting format it is to work and create with.

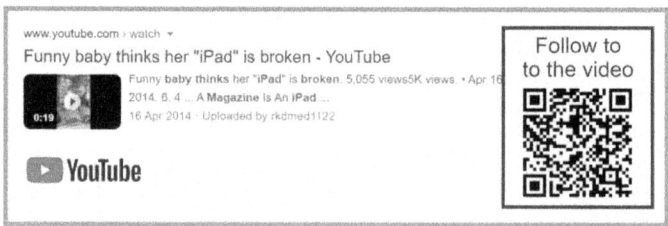

Figure 5: There is more power behind print than just being treated as a broken iPad

Chapter 1
Surprise – do something unexpected
Meet the needs of your customers and go beyond

We live in a world of expectations where we assume things will behave and appear in a certain way, because that is the way they have always done so. If we are surprised in some small way, it is memorable.

When my daughter was two years old, she took a punnet of cherry tomatoes and neatly restacked them into a pair of slippers. Who said cherry tomatoes needed to be kept in a punnet? For my daughter, the slippers were the perfect place to put them. A chef might disagree but it wasn't up to a chef, it was up to a 2-year-old. By presenting the cherry tomatoes in a red slipper, instead of a plastic punnet, my daughter created a surprise and turned the mundane into a memorable and remarkable item.

> *Presenting a marketing message in an unexpected way, will create a surprise and spark interest.*

All it takes to create a surprise is to do something unexpected. When people are surprised, they pay more attention and, therefore, remember. Presenting an otherwise unremarkable marketing message in an unexpected physical format will create surprise and spark interest that is independent from, but will draw attention to, the graphic design or marketing offer.

This chapter will outline a systematic approach to firstly identify what people expect to see when it comes to print and then discover opportunities for doing something unexpected with the physical form of print, thus creating a surprise element and increasing the effectiveness of print as a form of communication.

Dimensional prints

The US Postal Service (USPS) conducted a study in 2013 called, 'Enhancing Mail for Digital Natives'. They used 2 focus groups aged 16 to 25 to gauge reactions to current well-designed printed pieces. They presented the groups with two sets. The first set used standard sizes and paper stocks. The second set was multidimensional and used thicker stocks, custom shapes, bright colours, pop-outs and holograms.

The response to the multidimensional print set was overwhelmingly positive. Some participants said they would keep the piece, not for the content of the message but for the innovative features. They responded that a company that printed innovative pieces would be seen as trying harder to be 'new age' and progressive.

Doing something unexpected with the physicality of the print will lead customers to view the brand business and the products in a more positive light and they are more likely to keep promotional pieces for longer.

Retail experience

A visual display is often a customer's first contact with a brand. This may occur while they're walking past shopfront and instore displays or through car graphics or posters. Research shows that most buying decisions are not planned but are made at the last minute as the customer reaches for the product. The customer may already have a need but are yet to choose a brand to fulfil it.

The major aim of visual merchandising; for retail is to draw customers into the store or entice them to interact with the brand. The retailer wants the customer to extend their stay in the store or stay in contact for longer therefore being more motivated to buy. Simply put, a customer is more likely to purchase from you if they are in your store looking at your products.

Nirma University in India conducted a survey of 385 customers as they exited a retail furniture store. The results showed it was the window display that caught their attention and brought them into the store[5]. Visual merchandising (VM) displays have many elements and often rely heavily on print for backdrops, props or product and pricing information.

The University of South Africa study[6] of VM for apparel retailers produced similar results. Their exit surveys showed the window display and storefront were the best ways of getting customer attention and bringing them into a store. A similar study[7] published on sciencedirect.com was carried out with footwear retailers in Lithuania and produced almost identical results. Both studies found that the VM displays in storefront windows brought customers into the store, subsequently making a purchase.

In 2016, in direct opposition to these findings, Gap CEO, Art Peck, told analysts, 'I think windows today are much less relevant than they have historically been and you will see this going forward – that we are actually 'skinnying down' our window treatments.' He had come to the conclusion: 'If you haven't won at the digital interface on the front end, your window in the mall store is probably not going to make a difference at the end of the day.' That year, Gap's turnover was down 12% while, in the same period, the S&P 500 for the rest of the country rose by 23%[8]. This shows that retailers cannot afford to ignore their window displays and, by extension, cannot afford to disdain the print medium in their marketing.

Limiting factors

There are some common reasons things are the way they are in print.

Cost is a common limiting factor. Marketing budgets are typically limited and not every great idea will fit into the budget. The result is that a lot of the print marketing is done within a range of common sizes because print production economies allow for lower costs within that set of sizes.

Then there are the practical realities of each customer's capabilities, fittings or existing infrastructure. If a customer cannot easily accommodate a print, they are more likely to quickly dispose of it, which you do not want. Consider the environment the print is entering and how it can enter and remain in that environment for as long as possible.

Let's look at business cards as an example. The world has evolved to support the standard business card size of 90 mm by 55 mm. The design of business-card wallets and desktop card-holders accommodates standard-sized business cards. Oversized cards won't fit and will probably end up in the bin. Undersized cards will be lost inside the holder or wallet, never to be seen again. In either case, nonstandard sizes fail.

Another example could be a customer's existing onsite fittings. For example, when framing posters, the poster must fit the frame; wall graphics must fit on space on the wall; when hanging a sign, there may be head clearance considerations so people can still walk under the sign; freight providers will have requirements for the dimensions of the packages they will carry when distributing your promotions.

Another consideration is a print the customer may need to carry around, like a map or a worksheet – how they will use it, carry it and store it for later use are well worth thinking about.

Such parameters remind us that customers have particular needs in using and managing print. If those needs are not met, the printed object will fail as a marketing piece because it is in the trash.

The exception proves the rule

The various limitations combine to create norms that form our daily expectations for the physicality of print. It is important to know how to systematically define the various expectations and find ways to consistently go 'outside the square' and create a surprise. By understanding the limitations, you can then break them down intelligently and elegantly to create something unexpected. Once you've done this, you seamlessly enter the customer's environment and stay there for a long time – continually augmenting the graphic design or marketing message.

Rare shapes

With comparable messages all arriving in the same shape, an unusual shape can catch the eye of the potential buyer. For example, business cards are standardised and letters are mostly written on stock of the same size and shape. You have an opportunity to make customers curious, attract their attention and win their business by 'bucking the system' and being original in the form and presentation of your message.

In visual merchandising, unusual shapes can draw attention to the shopfront display and the product range, thereby helping lure customers into the store.

In a shopping centre, imagine a window sticker promoting a new range. The sticker could be made into an unusual shape that complements the visual merchandising in the shopfront. Many studies, including the 2 mentioned previously, have found window displays are crucial in helping increase foot traffic in a retail store. An unusual-shaped window sticker or rigid print could attract attention long enough for the customer to look at the rest of the window display, thereby potentially improving sales volume in your store.

Some examples of effective visual merchandising used for storefront displays include:

- Urban fashion retailer, W.Lane, created a window display with a life-size pop-up bicycle made from cardboard sheets. They added an original floor decal that looked like a cobbled pavement and complemented this with a matching backdrop banner.

Figure 6: W Lane window display

- Cotton:On Kids created a Halloween store display using unusual shapes to create hanging bats. These were hung all around the store, creating interest and increasing foot traffic.

Design a surprise

Putting a marketing message on an unexpected or unusual physical form will create something surprising and genuinely interesting to the audience. Of course, this can be done with clever copywriting, or eye-catching imagery. I propose it can be done more easily and more consistently with the physicality of the item. Fresh form and an original presentation will increase the effectiveness of the printed piece and its graphic design in a way that is only possible in print. No other communication medium has the ability to change its fundamental form. Powerful copywriting, stunning photography and eye-catching graphic

Figure 7: Cotton On Kids window display and visual merchandising

design are all very difficult but changing the physical form of print is easy, repeatable and effective.

Even a small shift from the usual will create an item that demands attention. When my daughter filled the slipper with beautifully stacked cherry tomatoes, all she changed was the container the cherry tomatoes sat in – from a punnet to a slipper – but she created something memorable and remarkable.

Doing something truly surprising with the physicality of a marketing message creates increased levels of engagement with your audience.

Managing costs

Marketing budgets are always tight and doing something extraordinary is often not cheap. When trying to make a project fit into a budget, the top three variables to adjust are:

- budget
- quantity
- size.

These three areas are the most important consideration when fitting a project to financial limitations.

Budget

Budget might seem an odd one to include because increasing the budget increases what fits within that budget. Print production works in economies of scale – the higher the quantity, the lower the cost per unit. For example, $500 will purchase 500 units but for $550, you can purchase 1000 units. Economies like this are common in print production and it may be that doubling the quantity is worth a 10% increase in budget.

Quantity

Print production is all about set-up costs and economies of scale. Therefore, there is great potential for savings to be found by investigating quantities you think may be required.

Get quotes on 3 quantities:

1. the quantity you want (Q)
2. double the quantity (2Q)
3. triple the original quantity (3Q).

Depending on the situation, it may also be worth getting a price on half the original quantity (1/2Q).

The range of quantities will provide an understanding of the pricing structure. You might find that triple (3Q) the quantity costs only a little extra, or even the same as the original (Q). There may be opportunities for efficiencies in a triple-quantity quote that you won't find in a single quantity quote. Don't feel bad about asking for multiple quotes; quoting 3 options on a single quote takes about the same amount of work as quoting a single quantity. Economies of scale are present, even in the estimating stage.

Another idea is to significantly lower the quantity. Marketers always think about print as a mass marketing tool but it doesn't have to be. It can be part of a highly targeted, personalised marketing strategy. In his book, *The Ultimate Sales Machine*, Chet Holmes[9] puts forward the idea of the 'Dream 100' – if you landed just a handful of your 100 perfect customers, it would change everything. With that approach – going after quality over quantity – it is possible to slash the quantity and open up production opportunities by spending more per unit.

I use this same approach with my business cards and frequently advise others to do the same. I get fewer cards per order and get high-production-value cards that use the same artwork each time.

Size

When buying print, it helps to think about it in terms of buying a weight or mass of paper and ink. There is a direct correlation between the weight of paper and ink you buy and the cost.

One visual merchandiser I worked with wanted to cover the shop walls with posters so she made up a size that was somewhere between A1 (841 x 594 mm) and A0 (841 x 1189 mm). Going above A1 in size requires different printing equipment and therefore entails a significant increase in price. I worked out that if we decreased the size by 5%, the cost would drop by 50%, which fell well within her budget. By being flexible with the size, we were able to bring her vision to life on budget. Size is the single most important dimension of print when it comes to price.

Where to start

Developing ideas for a 'surprising' printed piece will take time and research. You won't be able to send the artwork on Thursday, pick it up on Friday and use it on Saturday. However, the more you go through this process, the easier and faster it will be.

Begin by defining the norms for the kind of print being used and think about different formats. For example, think about all the door stickers you have seen in the past, focusing specifically on the variables of:

- size
- shape
- materials
- packaging.

Remember that these variables will not be relevant for every print promotion, so you should apply them as required.

Investigate each variable in turn by liaising with suppliers, getting quotes and contacting customers. As you collect information about production costs and learn about customer capabilities and infrastructure, look for ways to do something unexpected that creates a surprise. Remember, it doesn't have to be much to make an impact.

To help illustrate this process, I will take you through a common project.

Project

One thousand A4 letters, tri-folded and inserted into a DL envelope for delivery by the postal service.

Size

How big or small an object is forms the elephant in the room – it is beyond obvious. If you are designing a surprise, changing the size of an object is a reliable approach. However, when you are changing size, you will also quickly encounter various limitations. Generally speaking, bigger things cost more to produce, or at least more to move around, while smaller things get lost. Still, there is plenty of wiggle room between the extremes.

Letter in Envelope Project: the typical size of a letter is an A4 (210 x 297 mm) page, tri-folded into a DL (110 x 220 mm) envelope. Something unexpected would be to increase the size of the envelope or the letter.

The Envelope: a range of different envelope sizes are available, with some more common than others. The DL envelope is the most common because it is the cheapest to send. The C4 envelope (big enough to hold an unfolded A4 sheet) is about triple the size of a DL and quite affordable to buy and ship.

The letter: the norm is an A4 sheet, tri-folded to fit the envelope. Without changing the size of the envelope, you can send the letter as an A3 sheet (twice as big as A4). The A3 sheet will require more folds to fit the DL envelope. In turn, this requires more unfolding and creates a greater opening experience – as discussed later in this book, this is a good thing. An A3 letter will also create a 'lumpy' envelope, which is unusual in itself.

Next Steps: get prices for quantities of 1000, 2000 and 3000 A4 and A3 letters.

Also obtain prices for supply and distribution costs for the same quantities of DL and C4 envelopes. Alternatively, get prices for quantities of 500, 1000, 1500 and 2000.

Big letter

One industry body I worked with sent their letter as a 1.2 x 2.4 m rigid print in an effort to gain the attention of a federal member of parliament. They used the same letterhead and copywriting as a normal letter but the physicality of it was enormous. A regular envelope with a normal-sized letter was attached to the large print so the federal member could deal with a smaller version of the message in the usual way one deals with letters. Effectively, the large rigid print was part of the packaging and the message. They found an opportunity to create a surprise by doing something unusual with the delivery system, that is using a very large 'envelope'.

Shape

Shape is just as visibly obvious as size and is subject to similar limitations of cost and distribution. Anyone who has moved a fridge through a door, and then tried to get a lounge through the same door, knows this.

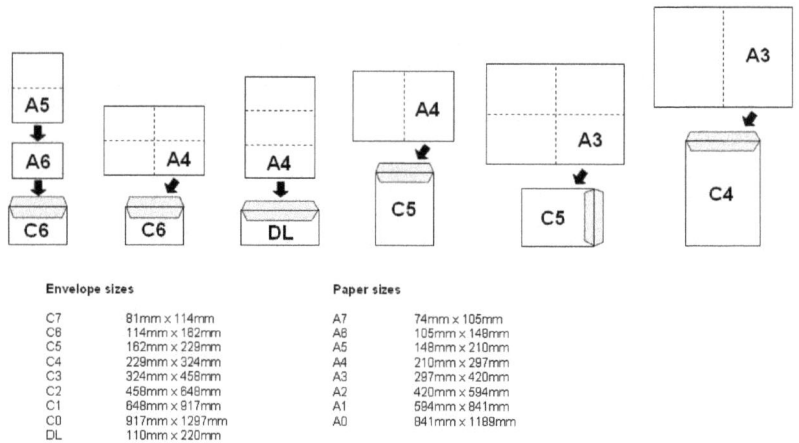

Envelope sizes		Paper sizes	
C7	81mm x 114mm	A7	74mm x 105mm
C6	114mm x 162mm	A8	105mm x 148mm
C5	162mm x 229mm	A5	148mm x 210mm
C4	229mm x 324mm	A4	210mm x 297mm
C3	324mm x 458mm	A3	297mm x 420mm
C2	458mm x 648mm	A2	420mm x 594mm
C1	648mm x 917mm	A1	594mm x 841mm
C0	917mm x 1297mm	A0	841mm x 1189mm
DL	110mm x 220mm		

Figure 8: Standard paper and envelope sizes

The common shapes seen in print are there for the typical cost of production and freight. In recent years, however, print technology has evolved so square-cut right-angle corners are no longer required for every kind of print. There are production processes that have moved away from using guillotines for cutting, to using laser cutters or automated cutting tables. These machines don't care if what they are cutting is a square or a circle and, in these cases, print production of unusual shapes may not cost more.

Letter in Envelope Project: typically, the DL envelope is a rectangle and the letter inside is also a rectangle. Changing the shapes could be an easy way to create something unusual.

The Envelope: there isn't a huge variety of shapes available in envelopes. It is possible to have custom envelopes produced but, even then, this is limited by the machinery to regular right-angled shapes. Squares, skinny rectangles like the DL and wide rectangles like the C4 are the only options. Squares would seem the obvious choice, however, that can complicate the letter production because of the need to fit. A C4 would be easier as the existing A4 sheet will fit right in.

The Letter: because the letter arrives in an envelope, it needs to be folded to fit. Folding is a rich field, with many interesting and engaging options beyond the basic tri-fold.

One fold, called a 'twist fold', can take a rectangular sheet and fold it down into a square. To open, the paper is pulled at the corners, making it spin and open in the hands. It's fascinating to watch this happen and just as interesting to try and put back together.

Figure 9: Opening a page folded with a 'twist fold'

Next Steps: in the previous steps, you gathered prices for the C4 envelope. Now, you can also get prices for a square envelope in the same quantities. Obtain pricing to print a normal A4 letter and a twist-folded letter, again with the same quantities.

Pineapple mailer

A fashion label I worked with sent out one marketing message with crepe paper pineapples, in line with their retail shopfront displays. The pineapples folded down flat for shipping, then expanded into a colourful three-dimensional fruit. One pineapple recipient told me their 'pineapple' had become an office celebrity. It had been given a name and lived in the office for months, moving around, starring in practical jokes and featuring in social media feeds.

The fashion label saw an opportunity to put a paper pineapple in their campaign. Folding flat meant each unit was very economical to distribute and elegantly navigated financial and freight limitations. By sending their message in a surprising way, on a 3D crepe paper pineapple, they transformed a mundane marketing message into a message that was novel and engaging.

Figure 10: 3D crepe paper pineapple

Materials

What materials to use is actually a huge question and will be discussed in depth in the Value and Experience principles in Chapters 2 and 3.

The materials used in any print project speak for themselves, each carrying their own implicit meaning. Doing something unusual with the materials is a very easy way to convert the mundane into the extraordinary.

The envelope: the average DL envelope is a lightweight, 70 gsm uncoated white envelope and is very common – therefore it is easy to do something unusual. Coloured envelopes in standard sizes are easily obtainable and eye-catching in a pile of white envelopes. Rigid envelopes made out of a light cardboard are also available and will stand out in a pile.

The letter: the norm is an 80 gsm copy paper. Again, this is very common and easy to stand out from. Using heavier paper will make you stand out and also has the effect of raising the reader's perception of the brand and the offer. Another way to stand out is to use the same paper but cover it from edge to edge with colour – effectively making it a coloured paper. Actual coloured paper can be hard to source but using a flood background colour is easy and won't cost more.

Next steps: get prices on coloured envelopes and prices on letters with full ink coverage. Also, obtain prices on a typical paper weight (80 gsm) and a heavy paper weight – I would recommend 250 gsm or more to fully leverage the reader's increased perception of the brand. A slight increase in weight will largely go unnoticed, whereas a big increase in weight will be noticed.

Handpainted

An Aboriginal land rights organisation sent a unique petition to the Federal Parliament. The petition was typed on paper, signed and glued to bark that was handpainted on the surrounds, as with traditional works of art from that particular area of the Northern Territory. The presentation attracted national attention and helped pave the way for decisions on land rights throughout the following decades. The organisation maximised their opportunity by doing something different with the material the message was printed on, which not only stood out but was also congruent with their message.

Packaging

Packaging is about the box the goods arrive in. For many products, the packaging may be the only opportunity to use promotional print. For example, if you sell apples, the box they arrive in might be the only packaging used. While it is possible to use plain apple boxes, it is also an opportunity to create a surprise by printing something on the box.

What use might a carton have after the product has been delivered? Can you design your carton so it can easily be turned into a cardboard car or robot torso for a child? Perhaps you could include directions for how to turn it into a worm farm or a composting project?

Technology, such as QR codes, can link to your website with written instructions or an instructional video for assembling the item, creating an educational experience. If your item is sold in a shop, you can help close a sale with content on carton integrations. Integrating customers with your internet marketing system will help you interact with them and provide additional opportunities for gathering data and for influencing customers to buy more.

Toblerone

Figure 11: A unique use of a QR code made Toblerone stand out amongst competitors

Toblerone UK ran a campaign in 2019 that put a unique QR code on each bar. After scanning the QR code with their phone, consumers were able to record a personalised video message for the person to whom they were giving the chocolate. The recipient scanned the same code to view the message, which they could share on social media.

Packaging can thus be enjoyed and experienced by customers as well as the product contained within. You can create more opportunities to connect with the customer and remarket through online channels.

Letter in Envelope Project: I have been treating the envelope as a part of the project throughout, so there is no need for an additional focus on it. The case study of Toblerone and my own focus on packaging in this theoretical project show that packaging should be seriously considered as a channel for promotional print.

Every campaign is different. If you work through each of the variables as I did, you will find opportunities to meet budget and create a surprise. It only takes something small to be surprising. The goal is to have the reader do a double take with the physical design of the printed piece, reassess it and fully engage with the message. If you can achieve that, then the piece has stood out and brought additional attention to the graphic design. The potential pay-off can be huge on the return on investment.

Case study

Torn envelope

An energy company in New Zealand planned a mail-out of DL envelopes with an offer for new customers to sign across to their services. The marketing team looked at the expectations of the industry and the medium – the classic DL envelope with a letter inside, delivered by the postal service.

The marketing team found their opportunity for subversion in the medium. They produced the envelope and inserted their letter but before dispatching them, they tore the last 3 inches off the end of envelope and on the letter inside it.

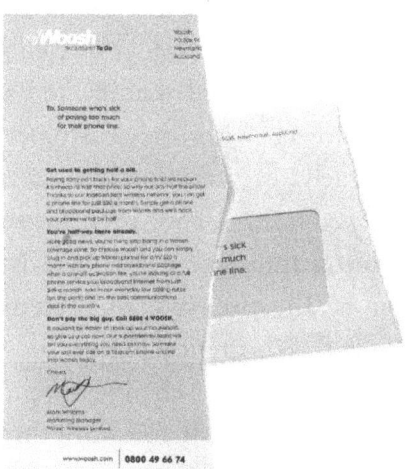

Figure 12: A deliberately torn envelope and letter added the perfect surprise element

Their graphic design allowed for the damage so none of the message was lost. When the customers opened their letterbox, sitting among all the neatly sealed envelopes was one envelope that appeared to have been torn open. The response was likely immediate, with thoughts of 'Who has been going through my mail?', 'What has happened to this letter?' and 'Who is it from?' The expectations for the medium were thoroughly subverted, creating instant engagement.

Using a nearby community, the marketing team tested exactly the same message in an intact envelope. The response rate to the torn envelope was more than double the untorn envelope. By simply doing something unexpected and subverting the norms of how envelopes look when they arrive, they increased the effectiveness of the campaign by over 100%. Surprising people with the physicality of print marketing, even a little bit, can have large results.

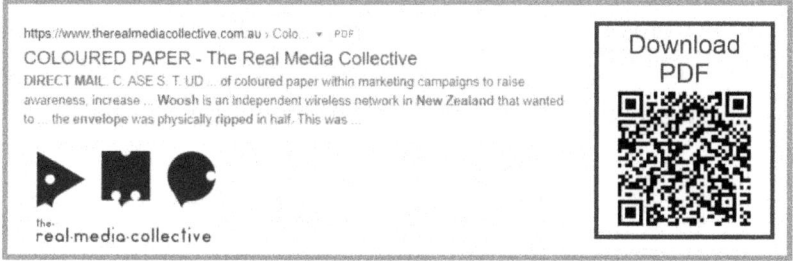

Figure 13: Find out more about the process and impact of the 'torn envelope' strategy

Key points in Chapter 1

- Surprise your readers with your printed piece. By doing something unusual with the physical form, you will increase its effectiveness.

- Your print campaign must be mindful of the practical capabilities of your customers and of infrastructure.

- The three most potent print production variables for getting a project within budget are: budget, quantity and size.

- Use nonstandard formats and stocks with custom shapes, bright colours, pop-outs and holograms.

- In materials, small physical changes from the norm can have an outsized positive impact on how your offer and brand are perceived by customers.

- You can design a surprise by systematically investigating the expectations of print and finding opportunities to create the unusual with the physical form.

Chapter 2
Value – make it precious
High quality produces better returns

A piece of paper in the office or at home is a problem that requires a solution. Decluttering expert, Marie Kondo, recommends getting rid of books as the first step to decluttering a household. Psychologist and bestselling author, Jordan Peterson, compares a pile of unopened envelopes on a kitchen bench to a dragon that needs to be faced, one envelope at a time if necessary. Unsorted paper is a problem and throwing that paper into the bin is an effective solution, especially if it's not needed – and no one needs a promotional flyer.

Every piece of printed marketing is going to end up in the bin. Throwing away an unrequested promotional flyer is as easy is clicking 'Skip Ad' on YouTube and feels just as good.

Stop people from discarding your print by giving them a reason to keep it: make it precious to them and create value. It is possible to create a piece so valuable it becomes a conversation piece but that generally doesn't happen. Most print marketing is on the short road to the rubbish bin. When I talk about trying to create value, the hope is to create enough value that people will hesitate to throw it away. When they sort their mail, they'll put it on the 'to keep' pile or, better yet, put it on the fridge, stick it to the wall or some other version of display. They decide that, in some small way, their world is better with your piece of paper in it.

Marketers typically rely entirely on graphic design to create value. They concoct a compelling offer, use interesting designs and imagery or list services that aim to connect with a need. That is good but it often doesn't create value. Creating value requires a different approach, which is closer to content marketing or helping someone buy rather than selling to them.

There is a second approach to creating value, achieved through recognising that print is a tangible physical object with height, width, depth and weight. The rules for making meaning are broader when using physical items. There are options to create meaning and value that no other communication channel offers.

It is possible to build inherent value into a printed piece that will give the audience reason to keep it or at least delay discarding it. The longer the message is kept alive and out of the rubbish, the higher the chance it will 'create' a customer.

Building value

It is possible to build value into marketing collateral in the following three ways:

- **Materials**

Make the piece valuable through the quality of the materials or the production processes used.

- **Utility**

Produce a useful tool customers will keep and use.

- **Content**

Create value by framing the item with information built around it or included on it.

Materials

Use quality materials to support your message. When using print, marketers often shop on price and look for ways to lower production costs. They see no reason to spend more on materials because they believe the value in the printed piece is entirely contained in the ink, that is the graphic design and copywriting. Imagine a panel beater putting a coat of paint on a Ferrari and claiming, 'Now it's worth something.' We all know a Ferrari has value, no matter what surface finish adorns it.

Humans are tactile animals

As a species, we have invested heavily in our brains and, by extension, our hands. Our hands have the highest concentration of sensory receptors in our entire body. Through our hands comes the tactile experience of the world. Observe any baby to understand humanity in its purest form – a person who inspects the world around them, partly with their eyes but more thoroughly by touching everything with their hands and then sticking these things in their mouths. It is no accident that, after the hands, the lips and tongue have the next largest concentration of sensory endings.

In the 1950s, American neurosurgeons, Herbert Jasper and Wilder Penfield, published groundbreaking research mapping brain function. They were able to identify which parts of the brain received sensory input from different parts of the body. This research led to the development of the sensory homunculus, which is a visual representation of how much brain tissue is devoted to each area of the body. It is a (grotesque) human who has been reproportioned in direct relation to the distribution of sensory nerve endings. The hands are enormous and the lips and tongue are also enormous. It is fascinating to see where humans have invested the majority of their sensory endings. Other animals invested in hearing and smell, while humans invested in touch and manual dexterity. Given these two sensory organs on the end of our arms, it is no surprise we can draw a lot of meaning and understanding about the world around us with our hands.

Figure 14: The sensory homunculus, which shows the distribution of a human's main sensory areas

The medium shapes the message

In 2015, Dr David Eagleman, neurologist and haptics (communication by touch) expert, investigated[10] the effects of paper stock on communication. Participants read fictitious company brochures that had been printed three ways: on heavy, high-quality coated paper, on lower-grade uncoated paper and on a tablet. The graphic design was similar for each one and companies were randomly assigned a medium for each participant.

The study found that those who read on high-quality paper understood and remembered the content best, by significant margins. Companies presented on the coated paper left the best first impressions and people were most likely to recommend those brands to friends. A week later, people still preferred the companies they read about on the high-quality paper, with name recall for those brands the highest by a factor of 3:1. The medium shapes the message.

Tony Fadell, Senior Vice-President with the Apple iPod Division and inventor of the iPod gives sound advice when he says:

Even if you have constrained resources, do not cut corners. People will feel it.

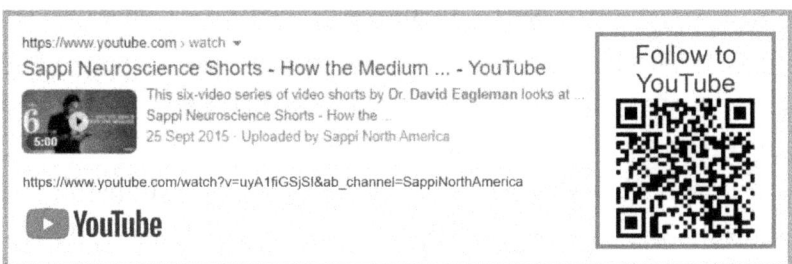

High-quality materials will generate a positive response from the customer. Quality materials in a printed piece will reflect well on the brand and the offer, imbuing the item with value.

Conversely, low-quality materials reflect negatively on a brand. People readily notice the low-quality paper because we are highly familiar with paper. As children, for many of us paper was one of the first things we had mastery of and it has remained in our lives ever since. Everyone knows good paper when they hold it. Light paper will make the piece be perceived as unimportant, from a low value brand, and likely to be thrown away quickly.

By saving money on print production through using cheaper materials, marketers may end up costing themselves money through underperforming campaigns.

Marketers often do their best to spend as little on print as possible, using cheap materials, even though it will lower the effectiveness of the campaign. In comparison, when it comes to graphic design or imagery, marketers do not fear to spend by getting an image from Getty or pay for their own photoshoot. Yet, the lay person viewing a graphic design has no idea about the cost of graphic design or photography. It could be a quick snap from a smartphone or a painstakingly crafted shot – the viewer doesn't know, however, they will know low-quality paper. It makes no sense to spend money on something the viewer will not notice, while tightening the purse strings on things the viewer will definitely notice and form their opinions around.

I worked with one ASX-listed, multinational that did a photoshoot with a number of world-famous, highly-paid athletes.

The images were used in artwork for promotional material for an event. Part of the campaign included some flyers to be handed out on the day and they asked me if I could print them on thinner paper to get the cost down. I understand there are budgets to be met but at a certain point you need to realise that if you don't want your marketing collateral to be treated like rubbish, don't produce rubbish collateral. Toilet paper with a photo of the Queen on it, is still just toilet paper.

Thicker stocks

Thicker paper stocks make the audience perceive tangible quality as they hold it in their hand.

Ordinary copy paper weighs 80 grams per square metre (gsm). It is purchased by the carton at the cheapest price for internal use. Everyone is familiar with it and knows its value. Double-sided print is typically done on stock that is 150 gsm – a familiar paper weight with low perceived value. People will feel the difference with paper heavier than 150 gsm. If you want to use thicker stock to make an impression and convey value, a minimum of 250 gsm will have real presence in the hand.

Business cards are printed on stock of 350 gsm and heavier. Paper stocks can become so thick, they stop being referred to by their weight in grams (gsm) and start being referred to by their thickness in micrometres (μ – μm). Printed objects using these extra-thick stocks feel as if they were printed on timber. I remember one customer described his thick business cards as cricket bats.

Figure 16: Plastic cord www.printonwood.com.au

Unusual stocks

Textured, coloured or patterned paper stocks can increase the value of a printed piece by providing a bespoke feeling in the user and a unique or at least unusual experience. These paper stocks are extremely useful for invitations, postcards, birthday cards, orders of service for weddings or funeral ceremonies, menus and certificates. The audience can tell the paper is unusual at a glance.

A paper stock with visibly recycled content can eloquently demonstrate a brand's environmental values.

Plastic stock is generally confined to producing credit and membership cards but is also readily applicable to business cards. Clear or opaque plastic business cards or invitations always stand out.

Figure 17: Square wooden card www.printonwood.com.au

Metal or timber business stocks are rarely but, if used, tend to typically be seen on business cards and wedding stationery. One of the few timber printers told me his work was his best referral source as people were reluctant to throw away a timber business card or invitation they had received and kept them for years. Eventually, they would contact him wanting to get their own timber printing done. People hold on to such prints simply because they are so unusual and valuable enough to keep.

Figure 18: Profile cut brushed steel card

If someone keeps your card only because it's unusual, that's good. The idea is to be noticed and remembered. Use materials to make the printed output so valuable that people feel compelled to keep it.

Magnets

Fridge magnets are unique among marketing collateral because they have a designated place to dwell – the fridge. The typical fridge is a busy place that is highly frequented by the occupants of the house or office. Any fridge magnet can be considered for a spot on the fridge. A good magnet is an asset to any household and could stay on a fridge for years. Unlike any other marketing piece, the fridge magnet can be judged by an additional standard – can it hold a piece of paper?

Regardless of the attractiveness of a magnet, its simple, but important, function will be appreciated. So, when using magnets as promotional collateral, add value and earn a place on the fridge by using a strong magnet.

Embellishments

An embellishment is an additional production processes that adds visible finishing touches to a printed piece, increasing its perceived value. Any print equipment can produce ink on paper but embellishing will not only increase appreciation of the piece but also the perceived value of your brand. Following is an outline of the many embellishing processes that will boost the aesthetics of a piece, taking it into the extraordinary and remarkable.

Embossing

Embossing is the oldest form of printing. The machinery has changed since the Gutenberg printing press of the1400s but the process essentially remains the same – raised or recessed relief images and designs are primed with ink and lifted above or pressed into the surface of the paper.

Certificates often incorporate embossing because no other embellishment communicates prestige more clearly. A certificate is a form of print marketing that must convey greater value more than any other marketing piece. Through good design and enriched materials, certificates acknowledge the achievement of the recipient and convey the esteem of the organisation issuing them.

Figure 19: Debossed business card

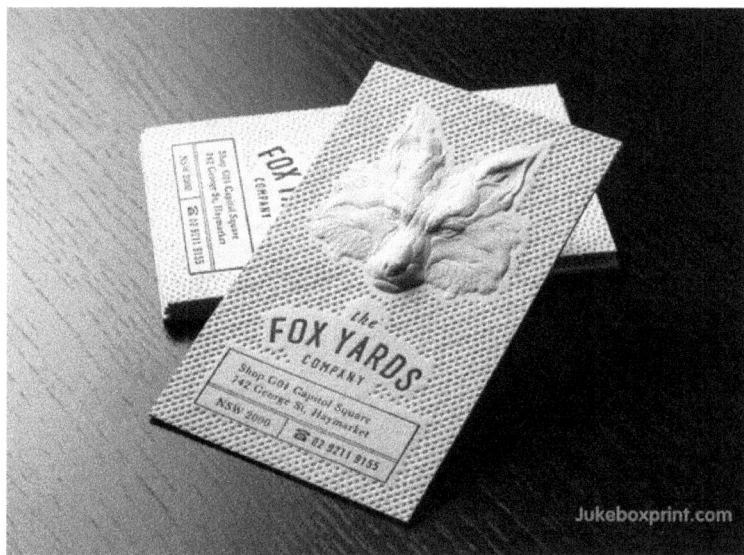

Figure 20: Fox Yards embossed business card

Foiling and Scodix

These distinct processes produce similar results. Foiling is a mechanical process that involves adding a metallic or coloured material to the printed surface and can be applied to solid panels, letters or filigree. Scodix is a modern foiling technique that looks like foil, but is a computer operated process, and can incorporate variable data in the finish. For example, mail outs or table cards, where there might be a hundred units, but each has a unique name on it. Foiling material can be metallic gold, silver, chrome mirror or bronze. Using a gold or silver metallic foil or Scodix recreates the appearance of precious metals and transfers some of that value to the printed piece.

Foiling is often paired with embossing, making the piece stand out with a striking, three-dimensional coloured effect.

Lamination

Also known as celloglazing, lamination is the process in which plastic film is applied to one or both sides of a printed piece. The laminate, which often fully encapsulates the printed object in the plastic, adds a layer to protect the print from the elements. A laminated print communicates semi-permanence because it is much tougher when compared with a normal piece of paper. Applying a laminate to any kind of printed object immediately increases its durability and perceived value.

Spot UV

This process can be done by a Scodix machine or through a screen-printing process. Spot UV is a gloss enamel, which is laid on top of the ink or lamination. It is often laid down as a gloss on a matt lamination, creating a striking contrast in finishes. Spot UV is a surprisingly subtle finish that is best used boldly.

Utility

People will keep a useful item

Print on a practical item can convert it into a valuable marketing tool. The promotional items field has exploded in recent years through the branding of items such as USB sticks, uniforms and coffee cups.

You can't drive in a nail with an image of a hammer on paper but many tools can be made from paper. For example, every IKEA store hands out paper measuring tapes. The production value of this item is low. It's not appealing or attractive paper but it's useful when shopping for furniture. Despite being a throwaway measuring tape, they often live on in handbags and glove boxes for years, keeping the IKEA brand as a talking point, visible and remembered.

Adding information specific to your business and relevant to customers to everyday items, such as calendars or notepads, creates a useful marketing message. Informative print marketing can distribute valuable reference material to customers and ultimately establish you as an industry expert and someone who can be trusted.

By converting a marketing piece into a tool, it will last longer, reflect well on the brand and be more likely to convert a prospect into a customer.

Printed items can have a long productive life

In 2015, Canada Post conducted an ethnographic study[11] into the routines of checking, sorting and attending to mail.

The study had two stages. In the first stage, participants wore eye-tracking headsets to measure the gaze and movement of their eyes as they interacted with the mail in their homes. The findings from the first stage informed the hypotheses of the second stage, which was a 2-week semi-structured online forum with diary entries. The study found that useful printed items were displayed in a dedicated area of the house (39%), kept for at least 4 months (20%) and often shared with other household members (35%).

Catalogues have a greater lifespan than any other form of printing. The Canada Post study found they were kept for up to 4 months. From my own experience, I know some catalogues can be kept for years, particularly for business-to-business catalogues, which are not prone to seasonal or periodic changes like business-to-customer catalogues are.

NUMBER	FACT
17 days	Advertising prints are kept for 17 days on average
40%	40% of customers keep catalogues for at least a month (20% keep them for at least 4 months)
66%	66% of customers keep prints they consider useful
39%	39% of customers have a dedicated print display area at home

Table 1: Summary of Canada Post study findings

Print at home heat map

The following heat map image is of a typical household, showing where prints were kept in the participant's home.

This study focused specifically on mail but I believe the findings are indicative of how print that is sourced elsewhere will

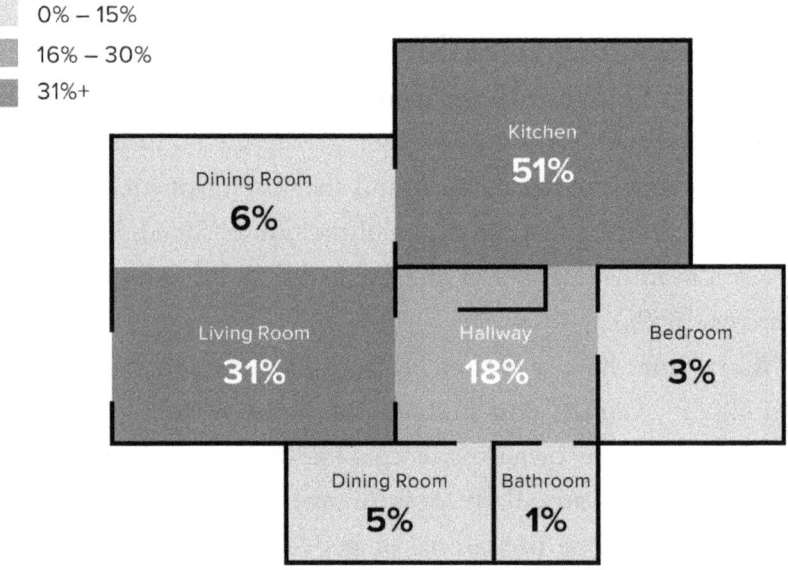

0% – 15%
16% – 30%
31%+

Dining Room
6%

Kitchen
51%

Living Room
31%

Hallway
18%

Bedroom
3%

Dining Room
5%

Bathroom
1%

Source: Royal Mail MarketReach, Ethnographic Quant, Trinity McQueen, 2014

Figure 21: Where are prints kept in a typical household?[14]

enter a household. Print typically cycles through three stages as it enters a home:

1. The holding area where print is kept before being dealt with
2. The pile where print is kept after being sorted and while awaiting action
3. The display area where useful or important print items are stored

From this study, we can conclude that useful prints will persist in high-traffic areas in a household or office for months where they will be shared with others, thereby increasing their chances of converting readers into customers.

Catalogues

Catalogues are a real stronghold for print and provide some of the most compelling arguments for using the print medium. Even the major online business, Amazon, has started using print catalogues.

Often, catalogues are used in direct-mail campaigns. As a result, national postal systems have conducted extensive studies into the efficacy of catalogues. In researching this book, I read many major studies of catalogues available from the postal services in the USA, UK, Canada and Australia.

Catalogues are highly valuable as reference materials. They enable customers to closely read what a store has to offer, free from the distractions of the screen. They particularly help those on a budget to plan their purchases before entering a store, either on the street or online.

A Roy Morgan survey[12] asked 30,000 Australians to rank the media they found most useful when making purchasing decisions. Catalogues ranked first across 11 categories, second across 4 categories and third across 3 categories. Grocery catalogues ranked as the most useful, at 52%, children's wear and toys came in the next most useful at 44% followed by alcoholic drinks at 43% and small electrical appliances at 41%.

Paper maintains our focus

Abigail J. Sellen and Richard H. R. Harper wrote *The Myth of the Paperless Office*[13] for Cambridge University to investigate why paper, as a format, is so resilient. They studied the role of paper in the workflows and habits of what they called 'knowledge workers' in the International Money Fund (IMF), conducting interviews and focus groups to learn why this business still relied heavily on paper.

Sellen and Harper found that people liked working with paper because they could use it in different ways. When authoring their own work, they would draft it on computer, print it out and then review it with a pen. They would also do the same with the work of colleagues. The user could write notes, bend corners of pages, place their finger on a page or surround themselves with pages showing important information.

This is relevant to catalogues because people can write on the catalogue, circle their favourite items, fold the corners on important pages and easily share them and show them to other people.

When using paper, we can quickly switch between various documents without losing focus. The internet opens up a vast amount of information and is unequalled in its capacity for distraction. In contrast, paper enables us to stay focused. It can operate as an anchor. A person might sit with a catalogue, then use their phone to research a product online and end up checking Facebook. When they stop using their screen and look down, there is the catalogue. It's still where they left it and brings them back to the product they were considering but had probably forgotten they had even been looking up.

A catalogue sitting on a table at home is highly accessible; studies show that people of all ages read and respond to the format. Compare an emailed catalogue to the printed version. Only one person will open the catalogue if they even respond and risk opening the attachment. Studies have shown that if you mail a printed catalogue to that same household member, everyone in the household, regardless of age, will read it. Catalogues are highly useful tools for the audience and generate rewarding responses from all ages.

NUMBER	FACT
55%	The percentage of main grocery buyers who purchased after reading a catalogue, leaflet or flyer in the past 7 days[14]
62%	The percentage of Australian mean who make special trips to buy after viewing a catalogue[15]
52%	The percentage of people who bought more than they planned when shopping with a printed catalogue[16]
87%	The percentage of Coles magazine readers who were likely to buy ingredients from Coles specifically for a featured recipe[17]

Table 2: How catalogues make readers respond and buy

Customers can readily browse the whole range of a brand in a printed catalogue and are likely to make larger purchases or buy products they wouldn't consider. Royal Mail Market Research reported that 52%[14] of people bought more than they planned when shopping with a printed catalogue. Roy Morgan found that 63% of women and 70% of men purchased more than they had planned after reading a catalogue[15]. The numbers vary a little from study to study but the general trend is the same. Print can give people easy access to the store inventory and will increase the cart size of around 50–70% of purchases.

Woolworths Fresh magazine is a free magazine available nationwide at Woolworths stores, and has a readership of over 5 million according to a 2019 EMMA (Enhanced Media Metrics Australia) report.

Magazine Manager, Nicky Harper said; "By solving everyday food dilemmas and providing engaging recipe ideas, tips and advice that inspire our readers to try something new, 'Fresh' actively helps Woolworths customers get more from every shop.

"We are pleased to see that our readers are getting value out of the magazine, through authentic, attainable tips and high-quality recipes - all for free.

"Each month in the magazine, we take great pride in ensuring that all of our recipe ideas focus on the beautiful fresh in-season produce that is available at that time alongside healthier, easier and convenient meal options.

"Our readers can also learn about the latest food trends and how you can hack fantastic food products that are available in the supermarket and make the dish your very own."

Figure 22: Woolworths 'Go Fresh' magazine

A business-to-business brand can supply their business customers or resellers with unbranded product catalogues without pricing. In that way, resellers can use the catalogues as a sales tool. An extension of this idea is to create supply resellers with their own branding on the catalogue, potentially at a price.

Worksheets

Venues and event managers often provide their visitors with worksheets to use. How the customer will use and store the worksheet must be considered when designing these pieces. The goal is to have them keep the piece as a memento or valuable reference item, not throw it away or lose it in a set of shelves. Convention organisers will often hand out useful worksheets in a mix of sizes and with no way to store them. In the venue, A3 posters might be nice to write on but to get them home they need to be folded, meaning they're not a poster anymore. Keeping the sizes a consistent A4 allows people to take those prints home and use standard folders to store them together. Over a multi-day event, you might direct the visitors to buy a folder, perhaps from you, and fill it with the sheets they collect throughout the course.

Stationery

Good marketing targets decision-makers who often work at a desk in an office, so stationery, such as notepads, can be useful in print marketing. Notepads can even stretch to desk-pad size (A2). Every office worker uses notepads; they are generally well received by customers. For some customers, promotional desk pads become highly valued items. One customer I know would invite the product marketer to visit in order to receive more desk pads! That is a success story for any marketing piece seeking to be a useful tool.

Calendars

Wall or a desk calendars can be useful, especially when directed at a specific industry, to highlight industry-relevant dates or your own events. Accountants can put in reminders for when tax statements should be done; grocers might list seasonal fruits and vegetables.

Adding such relevance will distinguish your marketing from a generic calendar. The extra information will make the calendar a more useful tool, meaning customers will be more likely to keep and use it. One client of mine numbered the weeks of the year for their internal systems. I designed some promotional desktop calendars that reflected their numbering system. It actually helped them keep track of their own internal system and the calendars were sought after. A small change made these calendars useful. The customer would contact me towards the end of the year to ask for them to be sent.

Stationery is big part of any business and it can readily create useful items to give to customers or use in your office.

Schedules

Schedules are useful to the customers of a business that has class times or specific availability times. For anyone who attends regular classes, a simple timetable is an asset to keep on the fridge and is handy as a reminder or to add or skip a class. This is especially true for parents who might be managing activities for several children.

A printed list of term dates or a class schedule can stay on the fridge as a reminder, long after a student's attendance had lapsed. The Canada Post direct mail study found that people often kept a useful printed item on display for months. A past or potential customer may keep the schedule on display and should they decide to attend a class, the schedule will help them reconnect with the business.

Reference material

Every business knows a lot about what it does but knowledge that is common in your workplace can be interesting and educational to customers. Leverage this information and focus your marketing on educational reference material. For example, a building inspector could send a checklist that homeowners could use to help them assess a house they might buy or even to review their own home, should the time come to sell.

When I was growing up, my home had a magnet flyer from a local pest control business on the fridge. Printed on this flyer were 8 photos of dangerous spiders, information about them and emergency phone numbers, including the pest control company. It was an excellent resource for a young family living where some of the deadliest spiders in the world were seen almost daily.

That flyer lasted for around 15 years. It outlived two fridges and probably even the business that published it. I can still see it in my mind's eye as it faded and grew stained over the years. However, despite being worn, every time it was knocked off the fridge, it was picked up and carefully replaced. We weren't about to lose that information – it might save a life in our family.

Many years later, I advised a doctor I worked with to do something similar. We produced a magnet flyer designed to be a phone directory filled out by the user to list emergency and other important numbers. There were spaces for essential phone numbers that are common in every home: parents, dentist, police and, of course, the doctor's number, which was prefilled.

The reference material doesn't have to be completely connected to the brand; the customer will keep the print, regardless of the 'publisher', provided the information is useful. As another example, pool supply shops could produce the resuscitation signs that pool owners are legally required to display, and add their branding to it.

Creating content for reference material is easy. Every day, businesses get asked the same dozen common questions, the answers to which are valuable to customers. Listing those FAQs with their response is a simple way to produce quality reference material for customers who might keep the print on their fridge for years.

Tim Martin (General Manager, Media, Roy Morgan Research) summed it up when he said:

In a media landscape that often just assumes people are turning to the internet for information when purchasing or selecting any product, catalogues in fact lead the way for more than 12 million Australians.

Shopping list

Most people go shopping without a list and most shopping trips aren't planned. Studies investigating the percentage of purchasing decisions made while in the store have produced varying results:

- Point of Purchase Advertising International (POPAI) cites 70% (1995)
- OgilvyAction says 40% (2008)
- Independent studies show that 75% of all brand decisions are made at the point of purchase and 49% of advertising seen at the point of purchase has a direct impact on sales[16].

This means the timeframe in which a shopper is standing in front of a retail display, making that final purchasing decision between specific products, is a lucrative opportunity to influence shoppers' buying decisions with print. Store staff are not always available to attend to these critical moments but print can be there all the time. Informative printed material on shelves and around a retail store will staff the store with 'silent salesmen', informing shoppers about goods and services through printed messages without requiring staff to convey such information.

A 2012 study for the International Journal of Retail Management and Research (IJRMR) into the effect of visual merchandising on impulse buying found that promotional signage significantly influences behaviour and there are significant relationships between consumer impulse-buying behaviour and instore promotional signage[17].

Note that for mail-outs or other forms of take-home marketing, such as flyers, 39% of households display important paper messages in the home, generally in the kitchen, providing many opportunities for all members of the household to interact with the brand[18].

Figure 23: Print in visual merchandising at JB Hi-Fi

Content

Highlight the items you want noticed

Value can be added by framing information, that is, by using graphic design to show its importance. For example, you can highlight a phone number for normal enquiries that might also be used by customers for after-hours calls. Even if it is the working hours contact number, frame that phone number in the graphic design as an after-hours number and say something like 'Call this number 24/7'. It is not untrue or misleading, it is simply highlighting part of the service and creating value. Customers are less likely to throw away a phone number that could be vital for after-hours emergencies, so the piece remains in circulation.

Pleasant surprises

Handing out discount vouchers that are valid for a single day has been found to be particularly effective in retail stores. Professor Carrie M. Heilman from the University of Virginia conducted a study called *Pleasant Surprises: Consumer Response to Unexpected In-Store Coupons*[19]. Researchers intercepted customers entering two grocery chain stores, screening for those who had a shopping list of at least 15 items and were planning to buy from the targeted product range. No mention was made of a discount coupon at that stage. A total of 192 customers qualified. Half were give discount coupons for items on their shopping list; half were given nothing and were the control group.

The researchers found the customers who received the surprise discount coupons spent more and made more unplanned purchases than the members of the control. The conclusion was that an unexpected offer elevates the mood of the recipients, which leads to increased spending on unplanned items bought as treats.

Specifically, the data showed a $1.00 surprise discount coupon led to an increase of $7.68 in unplanned purchases. That is a 768% return on investment – simply by giving a shopper a relevant discount at the right time.

Discount codes vs 'sale on now'

A flyer that says 'sale on now' is informative and motivating but the audience has no reason to keep it for long. Discount offers and codes can readily make a printed piece valuable. Managers of brands that use this tactic have told me that flyers with discounts can keep bringing customers in for years. One business had such a flyer return five years after distribution. The flyer had been sitting on a fridge, waiting to be used all that time.

You can create monetary value in a flyer with an instruction like, 'Present this flyer to receive a discount' or 'Enter this code while checking out and receive a discount'. Suddenly, the flyer has a real monetary value. If the offer said: 'Receive $100 discount on your next purchase if you present this flyer', it is equivalent to a $100 note. This is pure framing; a generic 'sale on now' and 'present this flyer' or 'enter this code' can all work for the same offer. The difference is that the flyer itself has value for the latter two messages, whereas 'sale on now' does not.

Discount codes or vouchers also give the marketer valuable access to activity tracking, which is discussed in Chapter 5.

Scarcity

Harness the market forces of supply and demand to create value through scarcity. This tactic is mostly used for printed works, such as posters or art prints that will be sold directly to the customer, not given away.

A musician, for example, might create two kinds of posters to sell at a concert. One will be mass produced and sold cheaply, while another style will be printed on high-quality paper and promoted as a limited edition. A common way to do this is to handwrite a number on the bottom of the poster.

Art galleries do something similar with limited-run multiples of a printed work of art. Limited-run posters are, likewise, sold at higher prices. In print production, it is just as easy to produce 1000 posters as 100. Producing limited runs is a calculated decision to balance sales volume with retaining the unit price.

Making it clear to customers that a print is part of a limited run can increase its value and give the audience a reason to keep it.

Loyalty cards

A café card recording coffee purchases, for example, is another way of providing a discount. These cards help retain customers; they show that well-planned discounting can encourage customers to value and keep any marketing collateral that saves them money. Some interesting research has been done into the effects of loyalty cards on consumer behaviour. Further detail is provided in the article linked below. There are a few very simple tactics any business can use to quickly increase the return on loyalty card systems.

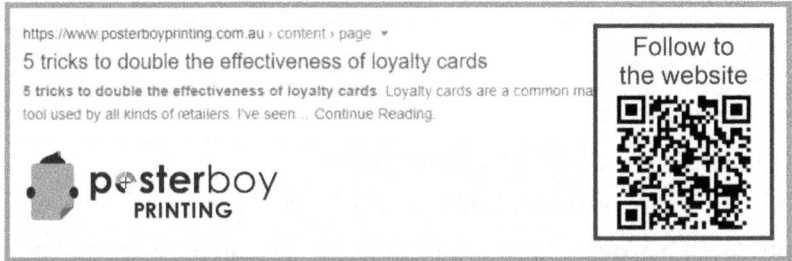

Figure 24: Scan the QR code to read more about making loyalty cards effective

Certificates

Another way to create scarcity is to make a printed item difficult to obtain; this applies to certificates. Certificates are really marketing pieces that act in three ways by:

- advancing the organisation issuing the certificate
- promoting the award, qualification or achievement
- benefiting the recipient of the award.

A good certificate can be a conversation piece. It can be prominently displayed for decades and the giver will be associated with the recipient. The potential longevity of certificates demands quality materials and good production value. In that way, value is created through scarcity and excellence, increasing the probability that the recipient will frame and display the certificate. Conversely, a certificate that doesn't measure up to the recipient's achievement is unlikely to be shown. It could be seen as an insult and will reflect badly on the organisation awarding the certificate. A different low-quality certificate might be gladly accepted and appreciated but will probably not be shown out of embarrassment. If an organisation wants to celebrate some exemplar, then they want the certificate to be displayed and they want the exemplar's profile raised in whatever little way they can. A certificate is a nice way to achieve this but it fails everyone if it is so cheap the recipient doesn't show it.

A good certificate starts with high-quality materials and production processes that imbue inherent value in the physical form.

Phone numbers

Details can add value to a printed item. Brands can frame contact numbers with phrases such as '24-hour service', 'In case of emergency, call this number' or 'after-hours contact'.

Another tactic is to include direct numbers on a personal business card. When the card is handed over, a simple statement such as, 'This is my personal number and is not on the website' increases the value of the card through scarcity, conferring privilege on the recipient of the card and giving the customer a reason to keep your printed piece, in this case, a business card.

Case study

The Nobel diploma

Not all achievements are equal, of course, nor are the paper certificates that recognise them. When an organisation produces a certificate, the physical form of the certificate and the quality of its production express the value of the recipient's achievement.

If a local organisation hands out a monthly certificate of appreciation to a member, the purpose is to give that member a brief acknowledgement. There is little expectation the certificate will be more than a simple print on copy paper from a desktop printer. But other certificates, on the same-sized paper, are given out for much larger achievements. People who have completed degrees or doctorates, or who have won Nobel Peace Prizes, expect more than a simple plain-paper acknowledgment.

Every year, the Nobel Foundation gives out 5 prizes 'to those who, during the preceding year, have conferred the greatest benefit to humankind'. The prize is commemorated by a medal and a certificate. The Nobel Prize comes with perhaps the most widely-respected certificate in the world; its high production value is unmatched.

The certificate, called a diploma, is on two pages. The material is parchment (treated leather), the letters are handpainted by a calligrapher and then monogrammed with gold leaf. Each diploma is unique. The Swedish text names the recipient and states why they received the award. The second page is a unique painting, influenced in style and content by the character of the laureate and painted by a leading artist. The parchment is mounted on a gold-monogrammed leather folder. Finally, the prize is presented to the recipient by the King of Sweden.

Now, that's a certificate. The quality of materials and production process is world-class. If you got one of those for getting up in the morning, you would keep and display it, not because of the award but for the inherent value of the materials.

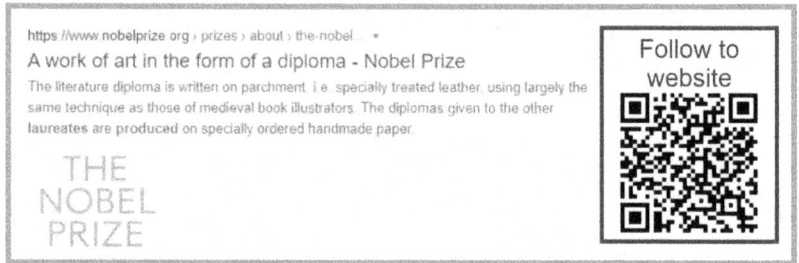

Figure 25: Scan the QR code to find out more about the Nobel Prize certificate

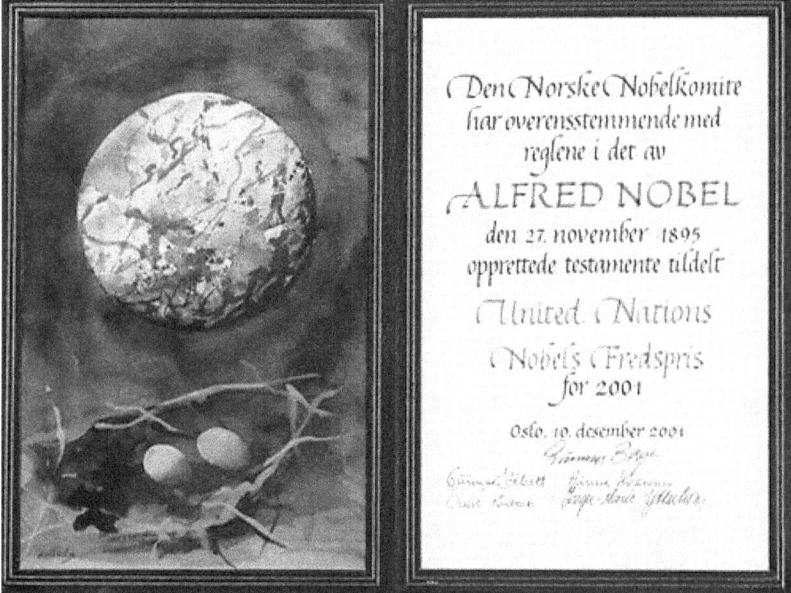

Figure 26: Nobel Peace Prize given to United Nations in 2001

Key points in Chapter 2

- By making the print valuable to your audience, they will keep it, thus keeping your brand in the conversation.
- The quality of the materials matters because of the experience it gives. Humans are tactile animals.
- Add value by making a printed piece useful, informative or financially beneficial.
- Consider your individual customer's world, how your print will enter it and what role it could fill to stay within that world. What value can it add?

Chapter 3
Experience – design the tactile experience
Ways to make print memorable

Consider your response when you receive a wrapped present. You pick it up, judge its heft, give it a shake and turn it to look at all sides. The wrapped package is an item unique in itself, separate from the contents. You will inspect it first before you unwrap it to discover what is inside. When you unwrap it, you have the opening experience that is common when opening an envelope.

As with a wrapped gift, we perceive a printed object as a manufactured item first and then as a communication. We investigate and draw meaning from the thing we find in our hands. Print, in contrast to every other form of marketing, joins us in the physical world with its weight, thickness, height and width.

Many modern marketers are digital natives who are so used to display-only marketing, they forget that, in some ways, communication in print is unique. Print can reach its audience through all five senses. The physical presence of a printed message is so obvious that marketers barely acknowledge the fact and rarely seek to design an experience or a communication just using the materials.

The paper used when making marketing collateral is more than just a vehicle that carries the ink. All aspects of the materials and processes used to produce a printed piece contribute to create a tactile experience that conveys meaning about the offer and the brand making the offer. Design printed marketing around the material to create a positive impression of your brand and inspire people, trigger an active response and increase the return on the marketing campaign.

> *In humans, touch represents a powerful form of nonverbal communication. Our sense of touch plays a fundamental role in daily life, from learning about objects to communicating with other people.*
>
> *– Dr David Eagleman*

Kids, paper and the power of touch

The brain consumes more than a quarter of the body's energy resources. Nearly half of the brain processes input from the senses, of which touch is paramount as the only sense that is distributed throughout the body. However, the sense of touch is not spread evenly. Our hands have about the same number of sensory receptors as the rest of our body from the waist up, excluding our face. Our hands are one of the most metabolically expensive parts of our body. The German philosopher, Immanuel Kant, posited that 'the hand is the visible part of the brain'.

Touch is vital in shaping what we feel. Using the sense of touch, the print medium allows us to craft a tactile experience, regardless of graphic design.

What we touch shapes what we feel

There is a heavy focus on sensation reflected throughout our language. We use terms like, 'a rough day', 'coarse language', 'smooth talker', 'the weight of the situation' and 'a soft touch'. There are endless examples of idioms couched in sensations we would normally process through our hands.

With our brains so connected to our hands, it should come as no surprise that we draw a lot of meaning through what we touch, consciously or unconsciously. In 2008, Yale University psychologists, John Bargh and Lawrence Williams investigated the impact physical sensations can have on interpersonal relationship. They gave their volunteers a cup of coffee, while they were riding an elevator for a period of 10 to 25 seconds, on the way to what they thought was the beginning of the examination. The coffee was either hot or cold. The volunteers were then asked to rate the personality of a fictitious person described to them by the researchers. Those who held a hot coffee consistently described the person as 'warm', showing that one brief physical touch influenced a completely unrelated judgement[21].

As a parallel, the tactile experience of wearing a shirt is not affected by the colour of the fabric or an image on the back but we do feel the cut of the pattern and the weave of the fabric. Similarly, a printed piece may be experienced through touch in addition to our visual response to the graphic design. The feeling of the paper stock and the shape of the piece constitute the tactile experience of the printed item.

In 2015, American neuroscientist, Dr David Eagleman, studied the effect of paper quality on communication. Subjects of the experiment were asked to read a company brochure on heavy gloss paper, light uncoated copy paper or in a digital format on a tablet.

The study found that those who read the brochure on high-quality paper understood and remembered the content best by significant margins. Companies presented on coated paper left the best first impressions and people were most likely to recommend those brands to friends. A week later, people still preferred the companies they read about on the high-quality paper and name recall for those brands was 3 times higher than for the least recalled medium[22].

Attract readers with a printed item's size and shape

Production techniques can create unique shapes and add tactile features to the surface as bumps or indentations that will attract the fingers and then the eye. Extending the trimmed size of one page in a booklet will call attention to that page. Printers can even add an attractive aroma to a marketing piece for added sensory attention.

The third dimension, absent on screens, matters. Print can create an experience that will capture the mind by designing a three-dimensional part that can be pulled out and assembled, or with directions on how to fold it into something useful or novel. It might be the components of a car that can be popped out of the sheet and assembled, or something like a kids' pop-up book that erects itself as the page is opened.

Digital experiences can be harnessed by print. QR codes, for instance, allow the audience to quickly access online audio and video libraries to complement the printed piece or send the content to your digital ecosystem.

Augmented reality has the capacity to change static images into highly engaging videos, instant-win games of chance or games of skill.

There are many ways to design printed objects to be more than the vehicle for graphic design. Printed messages can also be toys, tools, distractions or multimedia hubs.

Design remarkable

Print can be more than just ink. It can be something remarkable and fascinating. Business cards are a great example. People tend to want to pay as little per unit as possible and still get cards that are essentially the same as everyone else's. It doesn't make marketing sense. The idea of marketing is to stand out, not blend in. In my time selling print, the most common reason people get new cards isn't because they handed them all out but because something changed – a new phone number, new address, new logo, new staff member and so on. So, why spend less per unit? Spend the same total amount but get fewer cards. Spend more per card and have something remarkable that people won't throw away. Make a statement with the card. In our ultra-connected world, getting connected is easy. People don't need your card to get your details and once you've exchanged emails, your card is surplus to requirements.

This is not to say cards aren't useful. They are useful but today they serve a different purpose. Try this simple test: does your business card provoke a remark when you hand it over? Is it remarkable or, at the very least, does it get a double take? If your card doesn't provoke any kind of response at all, the customer has no reason to keep it and it will end up in the bin. If they comment on it, they will have reason to keep it floating around their desk and it will end up stored in a case.

Interaction is the end game.

The way to create a response like that is not with graphic design but with materials. Imagine two Ferraris – one red, one blue. They are still both Ferraris. The colour doesn't change that.

Renowned sales coach, Joel Bauer, has some very definite opinions on business cards. Take two minutes to enjoy his criticism of a business card.

Figure 27: Scan the QR code to find out what Joel Bauer thinks about business cards

There are a number of print material aspects to consider when designing a remarkable printed piece.

Tactile: What will users feel with their fingers when they pick up the printed piece? How does the stock feel? Thick or thin, smooth or bumpy? Have you used paper or a material that feels different, such as plastic or wood?

Visual: What will the audience see? What is the surface finish? Is it the flatter matt look on recycled paper or glossy on arctic white stock? What do the embellishments look like? Will people be attracted by metallic gold foil, a single colour or solid colours?

Smell: Printed objects can be made aromatic. What will users smell? Do you add a signature scent or one that accords with the campaign? Perhaps you're selling eucalyptus oil and your flyers can have a hint of gum leaf.

Do: What will users do with the printed piece? It could be a toy, a tool or something they can fold up or open out. Do you have directions on the piece for making an origami shape? Or could it be a paper tape to help people measure furniture in a store, similar to what IKEA offers to visitors?

Connect: Connect users of the printed item to your online content library. Send them to Spotify or YouTube so they can hear a musician you are promoting or play a podcast that explains the offer on the flyer. Link them to a video so they can place their phone on the magazine and the two can create a hybrid vision. You could use augmented reality to convert a photo of Kelly Slater surfing a wave into a video of the scene projected onto the shop window when viewed through the phone. Connecting is discussed at length in Chapter 4.

Tactile

Not all kinds of print will be handled but for those that will be, there is an opportunity to design a tactile experience. Give people an object their fingers find fascinating and their eyes and mind will follow. Sensory stimulation has proven benefits in retail – propensity to buy is correlated with the number of items people touch. Giving people a reason to touch, and keep touching, a printed piece, will move them closer to buying.

In a 2007 study[24] by Marc O. Ernst of the Max Planck Institute for Biological Cybernetics in Germany, two groups of participants undertook a memory task involving vision and touch. One group was presented with a visual pattern to remember, the other group were given the same visual pattern plus haptic feedback provided by a robotic arm. The device applied hard and soft sensations that were selected to match the visual patterns shown to the participants. The group that experienced the haptic feedback remembered much more.

The Royal Mail Service sponsored a study[25] in 2015 that used focus groups to discuss the effect of higher quality print on participants. Two marketing campaign prints were presented to the group, with two variations of each campaign. The first variation was a typical square-cut colour print on light paper stock. The second variation was of higher quality and used custom shapes, rounded corners, foiling and heavy paper stocks.

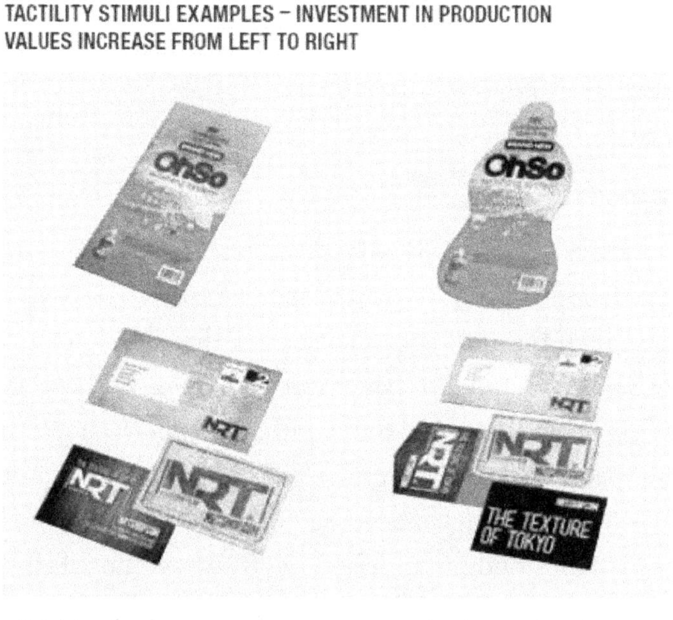
TACTILITY STIMULI EXAMPLES – INVESTMENT IN PRODUCTION VALUES INCREASE FROM LEFT TO RIGHT
OhSo
OhSo
NRT
NRT
THE TEXTURE OF TOKYO

Figure 28: Tactile elements increase perceived value with print marketing

As the printed piece become more stimulating to sight and touch, the amount of cognitive effort spent to create a memory of them dropped, and so a memory was made. This fits with research about how our brains work and is known as the 'cognitive miser' hypothesis. Simply put, we more readily remember things that feel unique. If your flyer creates a distinct tangible experience, it is more likely to be remembered.

Gain impact with paper stocks

Imagine you were given a range of business cards by contacts at a networking event. Most cards will be a 300 gsm or 400 gsm stock, measuring 90 x 55 mm – in other words, standard business cards. When leafing through your card collection, what if you found one that was clear plastic or metal? During the event, your fingers would gravitate to that unusual card because it felt so different.

What first attracts the fingers will next draw the eye and the mind.

Thick stocks

Heavy or thick paper stocks are an easy way to make your printed piece more interesting to the audience and to improve the perception of your brand.

The 2015 study by Eagleman showed that using heavier paper stocks had a positive impact on the audience's perception of a brand and helped them retain more information.

A 2013 study[26] by the United States Postal System used neurological studies and focus groups to discover how print could be enhanced for digital natives. They presented participants with printed pieces that featured embellishments, such as bright colours, pop-outs, holograms, heavy paper or unique shapes, or a combination of these aspects.

Both studies had near identical findings – the high-quality, higher weight paper was enough to improve the participants' opinion of the companies that were advertising. The foundation of the more favourable response was the heavy-weight quality paper stock, not the graphic design.

Using heavy paper weights will increase your customers' opinion of your brand.

Different stocks

Textured surfaces or coloured stock attract the eye regardless of the graphic design. Specialty stocks that are textured or coloured are often used for invitations, menus or orders of service at a ceremony; such stocks are often found in art and craft stores. This kind of stock is generally used for special community events, so it surprises recipients and attracts more attention in a business communication.

Even rarer are exotic stocks, which are available but seldom used. Business cards printed on stainless steel are a relatively recent innovation. This striking material can be cut to custom shapes.

Plastic can be used for business cards and other printing, as with debit and credit cards issued by financial institutions. As well, there is a printable timber stock – a thin laminate product suitable for business cards that can be used for any other kind of printing.

A printed object on such an exotic stock would create an immediate reaction from the user, who would focus intently on the material before responding to the graphic design. Novelty value would ensure attention as the materials make a statement of their own.

I frequently change my business cards to different materials because I like to use them as a showpiece for what other businesses can do with their own cards. When I used printable timber cards, people were fascinated by them. The thing that surprised me the most was people would actually smell the timber cards! I would often talk for some minutes, just about the material of the business card. This created rapport and easily segued to the graphic design and the message printed on the card. This is a resounding success for a printed piece.

Visual

Shield sticker

In cooking, they say the first bite is with the eyes. The same is true in printing. It is not initially about the graphic design but about the size, shape, materials and embellishments used. All of these things add meaning and value to the piece and create an experience for the audience.

To promote a retirement home BBQ event, marketers produced a folded flyer shaped like a hamburger (see Figure 17). They used a cross fold pattern so as recipients unfolded the piece, it was like deconstructing a hamburger. The cover looked like the top of a hamburger, the first fold revealed tomato, then cheese and finally, the meat patty. The patty was a removable circular piece that protruded on each edge through slits in the fold lines. As the piece sat open, it looked like a burger on a plate. The process of opening it was very engaging and the burger-shape meant people knew from a glance what it was about.

Figure 29: You can create instant interest in an event with an unusual flyer

Figure 30: Scan the QR code to find out more about the burger fold invitation

Intelligent use of creative sizes and shapes will add meaning to the materials used in the printed piece and provide a solid foundation on which to build your brand identity and message.

Packaging

A customer's experience of your product begins with the packaging. Why not turn your generic carton into a professional representation of your brand when the article arrives at your customer's door. Quality packaging can extend the experience of your brand, beyond buying, bridging the gap between purchase and usage. Beautiful packaging has a special charm, even for business delivery as it can create a moment of excitement and anticipation as the package is opened, similar to receiving a gift.

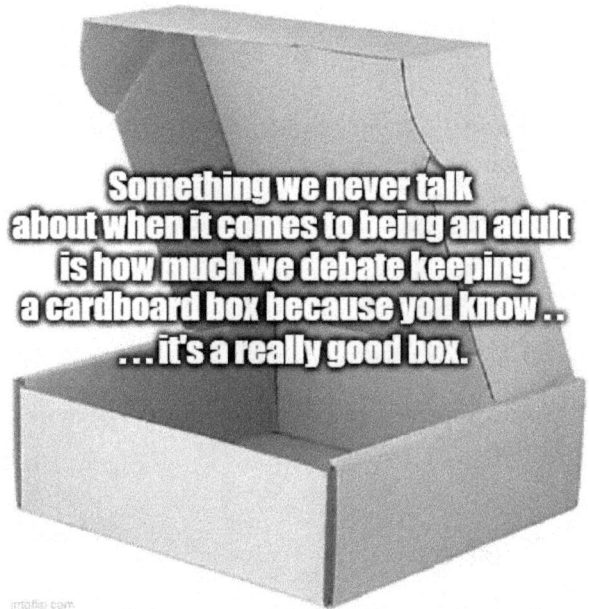

Figure 31: Packaging is an important part of the experience

There are growing opportunities for paper or fibre packaging to take over roles traditionally filled by plastic. L'Oréal recently changed to sustainable packaging, releasing a new range in bottles made from paper and clay, with a thin plastic liner made from 60% less plastic than previous bottles.

Most beer comes in paper cartons for six-packs, replacing the six-ring can-holders that have become a symbol of plastic waste. Such environmentally conscious packaging communicates the brewers' environmental values to the customer. Communicating brand values allow consumers to buy with a higher purpose or meaning than simple price or need.

Nestlé is working to replace all of its plastic wrappers with paper alternatives.

 Nestlé ✓
@Nestle

We are phasing out all plastics that are non-recyclable or hard to recycle for all our products worldwide by 2025, as we work towards a waste-free future.

♡ 43 3:12 PM - Sep 10, 2019

💬 20 people are talking about this

Figure 32: More companies are making the effort to be more sustainable in their packaging

Surface finishes

Consider the surface finish of the printed object. Production processes can create a bumpy surface that will interest the user.

The original Gutenberg printing press used a process very similar to modern embossing, which raises a design above the surface of the paper, and the negative form, debossing, which indents the design into the paper.

Other processes add a layer on top of the paper stock. As discussed in the previous chapter, these processes are called Scodix, foiling and Spot UV. They involve laying a varnish or a film on the surface of the paper, creating a raised area. The additional layer is thick enough to be felt by the fingers. These processes can also change the visible finish, creating a contrast that will attract the eye.

One client I worked with was a wedding and events organiser. He wanted to communicate a high-class, silver service look in their printed materials. On their business cards, they had been using a shade of grey to simulate silver. With the same design, we used metallic silver foil, which looks like polished silver. At a glance, even before looking at the design or reading the text, the piece communicated quality and sophistication in a way that grey ink did not.

Make scents

Sensory embellishments in marketing collateral are not widely used in Australia, but are much more prevalent in Asia. Our scent receptors connect directly to our brains for memory and emotion zones[27]. A familiar odour will stimulate the same brain tissues as memory and emotions, thereby translating 'inhaled molecular features into rich, emotion and memory-tinged perceptions'[28].

A 2015 market research study called 'A Bias for Action'[29] was conducted for Canada Post by Canadian True Impact

Marketing with the assistance of the Neuroscience Research Group at Copenhagen Business School and the Danish Research Centre for Magnetic Resonance. The study tested 270 participants in nine groups of 30 – one group for each media format. Each participant saw two offers (one from each campaign) on a single-media format.

Two integrated campaigns using mock brands were developed for this study – one featured a high-involvement offer from a travel agency and the other featured a low-involvement offer from a retailer. The same creative content and messaging were applied consistently across physical and digital media formats for each campaign.

The formats tested were ranked by their motivation-to-cognitive load threshold. This is a data-driven value. Advertisements that yield a motivation-to-cognitive load ratio of one or higher are considered the most predictive of in-market success, or likely to trigger the desired action from the consumer.

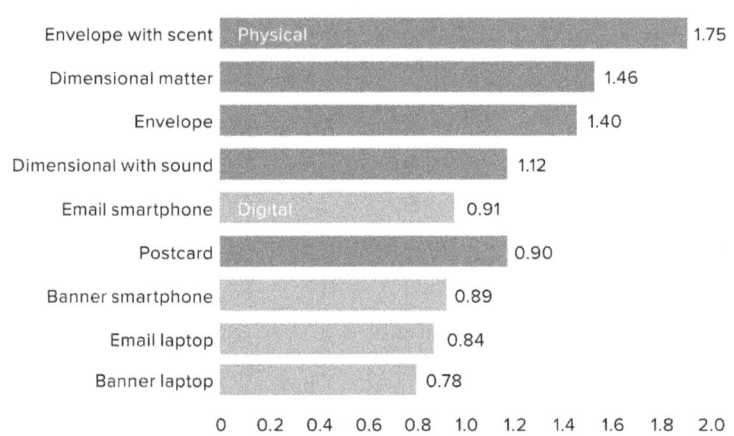

Motivation-to-Cognitive Load Ration — By Media Format

Figure 33: Formats tested in the 2015 'A Bias for Action' study

Researchers found that print media created a stronger neurological response, consistent with motivation to act. A high motivation score indicates propensity to pay attention and then respond actively.

The motivation score for print media was 20% higher than that for digital (6.77 versus 5.52) and 30% higher than the neuro-marketing benchmark for motivation (5.2).

True Impact Marketing founder and CEO, Diana Lucaci, said:

The extent to which physical [print] is motivating was both significant and surprising. For motivation, we usually consider a two per cent to five per cent positive difference to be a predictive indicator of future behavioural change. If, for example, you're choosing between two product packages and one generates a motivation response that is three per cent higher than the other, we can confidently say that choosing the package with the higher score will make a positive difference in the marketplace. And the higher the score, the more dramatic the behavioural effect.

The most effective and motivating of all the physical media were the scented items. Lucaci added:

Scent had a stronger impact on motivation but unlike the sound, it was not consciously processed. Participants had a better reaction to the piece verbally but couldn't pinpoint why. I think that's really interesting because scent has a tremendous impact on our lives. We expect certain scents in certain places, whether we're in our homes or at Starbucks. The scent gives us a feeling of being in a certain place at a certain point in time and it allows us to encode the experience into memory much more easily. It affects our whole mood, even though it's often so subtle that we aren't aware of it.

We are able to recall a smell with 65% accuracy after a year, compared with only 50% of visuals after 3 months. Put another way, in 12 months, a brand with a signature scent has a 65% chance of being remembered, while in 3 months, an unscented brand has only a 50% chance of being remembered. We might see or hear something that triggers a vague memory. Smell, in contrast, is like a time machine; a familiar smell can have a powerful effect on memory. When a scent reminds you of a holiday, a home or any particular place, you stop, close your eyes and are carried back to the original experience.

To get this effect in print marketing, it is not necessary to harness a smell from a customer's favourite holiday. Some businesses will have a characteristic smell that they can use but many won't. It doesn't matter – just select a pleasant scent and do your best to make it relevant to the campaign. If you can't, it doesn't matter. Studies show that simply having a scent on the print has an effect – a recognisable or signature scent is best but not necessary.

Do

Paper toys

Every day, in offices and classrooms around the world, someone crumples a sheet of paper and throws it into a nearby bin. Each time they do that, part of them is remembering being a kid – they aren't throwing something into the bin, they are taking a shot. They are playing. In other rooms, sheets of paper are folded into paper planes to see who can fly one the furthest. Paper can quickly become a toy that gives pleasure and so a marketing piece can become a toy the audience can have fun with.

Figure 34: An origami KitKat crane - a Nestle initiative

In Japan, the Nestlé company changed the wrapping material of the KitKat from plastic to recycled origami paper. Each chocolate comes with instructions on how to fold the paper wrapper into an origami crane. This idea creates many marketing benefits: involving the buyer, becoming a talking point, being re-used and echoing a Japanese cultural tradition. The packaging also appeals immediately and remains as a souvenir, developing attachment to the brand.

Figure 35: Scan the QR code to find out more about the KitKat crane

I use a simpler idea with promotional notepads for my business. I print a soccer ball pattern on the back of each page of the notepad so when a sheet is crumpled up into a ball, it looks like a soccer ball. It's an idea that would work with any sport-related ball and can be a way to tie a promotion into a sporting event or product or, as with mine, just for fun.

Opening experience

One of the findings of the Canada Post study, 'A Bias for Action'[1], outlined earlier, was that participants spent less time looking at the print media than at the digital media. This was paired with lower cognitive load while looking but offset by a higher motivation value. The combination suggests that the participant is getting the message faster and with less effort from print media. This is crucial because the less cognitive capacity spent on understanding a message, the more capacity for creating a memory and motivating the customer.

Participants reviewed a printed piece they called a 'dimensional mailer' – a folded brochure on heavy stock, similar to a birthday card. The dimensional mailer was the second most effective piece after the scented one when it came to motivating the reader. Being a folded piece, it offered the consumer an 'opening experience' to see what was inside. This would have involved opening the envelope, extracting the print and then unfolding it. This is a scaled-down version of the gift unwrapping experience discussed earlier in the chapter. It recruits more senses than simply handling and viewing an unfolded piece. The more sensory receptors recruited, the lower the mental effort is to engage, meaning there are higher levels of memory making and motivation. The study recorded a 60% increase in motivation between the dimensional mailer and a flat postcard that was the nearest equivalent in size and material.

Let me state that again – putting a folded card in an envelope is 60% more engaging than a flat card. That is the opening experience.

Wrapping or decorating with paper or other materials can convert a commercial delivery into a gift-giving moment. Car dealers, for example, use novelty ribbons to 'wrap' a new car before a buyer takes possession. The gesture elevates the transfer from a business transaction to something that triggers smiles all round. The opening experience can be harnessed for more than just envelopes. It's worth asking whether you can create an opening experience with your printed piece.

Can you go further and create a piece that can be shipped flat but folded in an interesting way – like the twist fold mentioned in Chapter 1 or a three-dimensional fold to make an object like the KitKat origami crane? Think of children's pop-up books that expand to create three-dimensional displays as the page opens, like the case study discussed in Chapter 1 with the 3D pineapple that helped to sell surf fashion.

Prints can now be cut into custom shapes for short print-runs, which makes it more accessible to more businesses, and allows for low investment experiments. This could allow you to experiment with optical illusions. Effects such as the anamorphic (image-distorting) illusions we see on football fields and pavement art create three-dimensional illusions when viewed from the right angle. Other illusions include the mind-bending distortions of the Ames Window, which could make an eye-catching window display and a fun inclusion with a mail-out.

One promotional mail I received a few years ago consisted of a heavy card stock that was cut in profile as a little car with the company's brand on it. My kids absolutely loved it; they poked it out of its paper frame and folded it into shape. My children loved it so much I rang the company and asked whether they would mind sending another.

This is a rich field. There are many free online templates of vehicles and animals. They are all three-dimensional models made from single-sided printed paper, cut to shape, folded and then glued together.

Hidden appeal

Coffee case study

Nescafé ran a campaign about sharing moments over coffee – 'It all starts with Nescafé'. They included their own conversation starter by inserting two foldable and usable mugs of Nescafé into a newspaper. The reader just had to add water and they had a two cups of black coffee to drink – carefully.

Figure 36: The 'mugs' of Nescafe as they were delivered

Figure 37: Ready to drink

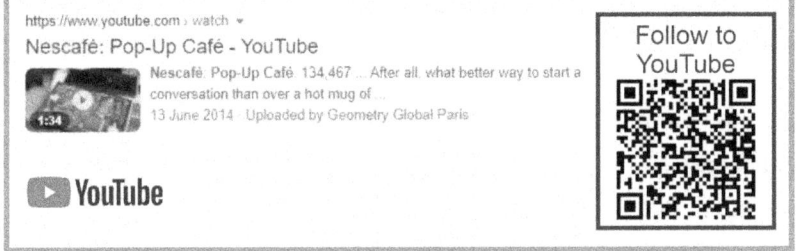

Figure 38: Scan the QR code to find out more about the Nescafe promotion

You will gain a positive response by giving the audience something more than a promotional message – they'll receive an item they can have fun with. This will reflect well on your brand, increase the lifespan of the printed piece and, with that, its effectiveness.

Say more

People spend very little time looking at online content; they filter through it very quickly. Consuming content through a screen is a comparatively rushed experience and limits the length of a message. The former CEO of Condé Nast, Scott McDonald, said:

> *When one is reading on the screen, it's sort of like speed reading, information-retrieval mode. 'I'm looking for something. Now I'm looking for something else.' It's very purposeful, it's very utilitarian ... There's something about it being on the screen that signals to people to hurry. It's pushing the page-down button, just having your finger on the clicker and scrolling. It's a higher speed, more nervous kind of thing.*

Screen-based reading, he adds, is 'very much about *search and destroy*'[32].

Some print is on display, such as posters or shopfront banners, and we see it only in passing. Other print comes into our hands, like catalogues, magazines and brochures, and we can spend as much time with it as we like. This tactile print, in all its various forms, has one thing in common – the audience has time to read it. There is no time limit or physical distance imposed by walking or driving past the message. Direct communication takes place between a brand and the audience, who have as much time as they like to dwell on the message.

Magazine readers show this starkly; they stay with the material for an average of 77 minutes, compared with 15 seconds for website visits and one second for digital banner advertisements.

Some products or promotions are easily outlined in 20 words or less but many could benefit from more. Print is a format that allows for more. Typically, more information is required when the unit price is higher or the customer is closer to the decision point. In these instances, the customer will want more details to support a final decision. The best way to communicate a lot of information is via the printed page.

In Abigail J Sellen's study, *The Myth of the Paperless Office*[33], one of the knowledge workers from the International Monetary Fund said, 'You've got to print it out to do it properly. You have to settle down behind your desk and get into it.' The phrases, 'settle down' and 'get into it', suggest a state of mind associated with a particular kind of reading – the full-immersion, deep-dive kind that occurs when a reader is able to shut out the world and truly focus.

Ferris Jabr explored *Why the Brain Prefers Paper*[34] for 'Scientific American' and found the physicality of paper was the driving force for human preference. Dr Eagleman and his students took these studies one step further by testing the quality of the paper. They found it was highly beneficial for recalling details and perception. Reading and writing leaves a greater 'haptic footprint' in the brain – it's that lasting impression that makes all the difference. The very physicality of the print creates an imprint on the human brain. Graphic design, photography and copy writing can build on this foundation and combine to create a highly engaging piece. The haptic footprint can be augmented further by adding an aroma to the print, engaging the sense of smell.

Direct mail enters the audience's home and is consumed at leisure in a relaxed and safe environment. This enables the marketer to communicate directly with potential customers, to involve and inspire them and to stimulate action. No other medium is as free of distraction as a printed item. Overall, 81% of Australians say they open and read their mail immediately and

74% pay complete attention when reading mail. There are no devices between print and reader. The emotional connection to paper and the tactility of catalogues help companies communicate vital brand messages. Creative design, copywriting, photography and styling combine to deliver a powerful message on paper[35].

The longer the audience spends interacting with a brand, the more likely they are to buy. This is especially important if you are selling expensive items. If the audience is considering a big purchase, they aren't going to make that decision without researching the brand and the product and print is an excellent format for finding out more. An Australian Direct Marketing Association (ADMA) study showed that print is consistently one of the top four mediums consumers rely on when making a final purchasing decision[36].

The pulling power and informative value of print can be exploited with pieces that will be useful at the end of the sales process. At this decision-making stage, customers want to learn much more about their imminent purchase. The best way to present this pivotal information is in print. Studies show that 56% of people trust information more when it's presented on paper and just before they buy is the moment you need customers to trust you most.

If you are creating printed communications, you can say more and be confident it will be read, understood and retained. These attributes mean the print medium can contribute significantly to your marketing campaign.

Catalogues

Printed catalogues are among the mainstays of print marketing. As consumers, we like to browse a catalogue. We are much better at browsing print than we are at navigating websites. A 2013 United States Postal Service study[37] used focus groups to look into ways of enhancing mail for digital natives.

Many subjects of the study said they looked forward to receiving catalogues and flipped through them when they arrived, searching for new products. Some mentioned that although they might find something in a magazine they were interested in purchasing, they were unlikely to go online and buy it. Subjects valued being able to scan a catalogue that would take them to additional information about a product.

For your marketing success, the best practice for catalogues, or any printed promotions showing many products, is to provide unique links for each product to take the print reader directly to a web page that provides more information and enables immediate purchase online.

This is covered by Chapter 4.

Aldi entered the Australian grocery market in 2001 and have grown strongly from a single store to over 500 around Australia making them on of the top 10 retailers in the country. Canstar Blue has rated them as the best supermarket 8 times in the last 10 years. Part or their success is through catalogue distribution. There are piles of catalogues at every check out, and each transaction concludes with the check out offering a catalogue. They have a constantly changing range of limited supply specials from tv's to ski gear and everything in between, using the scarcity and urgency tactic. It is all promoted through their catalogue, making the experience of getting the catalogue one of discovery, because the right offer could change your whole weekend.

Figure39: Aldi catalogue

Indexing

For booklets, a finish called 'indexing' makes one page wider than all the others, similar to a tabbed page in an index. A reader's fingers are drawn to the extruding index page and they automatically open at that page. This brings attention to a significant place, such as the 'sign here' page of a booklet calling for a response.

Print media, such as newspapers and magazines, can also use indexing to draw attention to your advertisement on a certain page. Of course, you would need to make a specific arrangement with the publisher to do that.

Indexing can also be achieved on a smaller scale using Post-it Notes. For example, if you have a small distribution of catalogues, you can apply a Post-it Note to a given page and include a cover note saying something like: I've highlighted a couple of pages I thought you might find useful. This is a simple way to create an experience with a printed piece and increase response by drawing the audience to the catalogue to see what has been highlighted for them. You may not even really want to sell them the product on that page but the idea is to design an active response.

Case study

Catnip wins the pet, then the owner

A Canadian pet supplies brand was opening a new store. To promote the opening, they did an unaddressed letterbox drop in the local area. Anyone who has owned a cat knows that the plant called catnip turns kitties into instant addicts. Cats become playful and actively roll around in the scent, drunk with pleasure. Many cat toys use catnip for added attraction. Cats lose all natural restraint and self-discipline as soon as they detect catnip in the air.

The pet supply business sprayed their flyers with catnip solution. When the flyer went into a cat owner's home, the household cat actively sought the source of their favourite smell, digging through the mail and pulling out the flyer. Of course, if you were to witness this, you would pick up the flyer your pet was so focused on to find out what was going on. It's that moment of interaction every marketer is after. The customer's cat was working for the marketer, presenting the flyer to their owner.

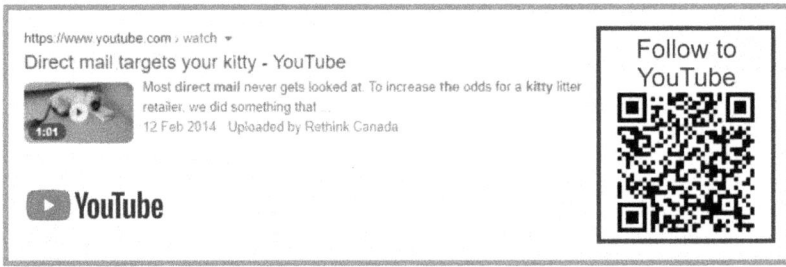

Figure 40: Scan the QR code to find out more about the catnip study

Key points in Chapter 3

- The feel of a printed item is a uniquely powerful quality of the medium.
- Through technology, as well as shape, size and even smell, print is unrivalled at capturing attention.
- Use print to create a tactile or multimedia experience.
- There is more to print that just the experience of the eyes; there is the experience of the rest of our tactile senses. Even smell can be harnesses to create a remarkable and memorable piece.
- Paper can be a lot of fun. Why not make your print informative, compelling and fun?
- Print doesn't have to be the end – it can be a means to an end. Design a piece that provokes conversation. The print is the means; the engagement and conversation is the result

Chapter 4
Connect – multiply traffic in the wider ecosystem

Multichannel beats single media

Print can be a valuable element of any multichannel marketing campaign because it has a multiplying effect on all other channels and increases traffic, both online and instore. To take advantage of this feature, printed pieces should be designed as a launchpad to send customers further down the marketing funnel and into the broader marketing ecosystem, using connection tools like QR codes, email addresses, street addresses, phone numbers, augmented reality (AR) or web addresses (URLs).

Steve Olenski, in *Four Key Principles of Cross-Channel Marketing,* says:

> *Successful marketers are nearly 35 times more likely to use cross-channel marketing with their customers versus under-performing teams who struggle to use this tactic at all[2].*

In 2017, Temple University's Centre for Neural Decision-Making in the USA conducted a neuromarketing study[3] to understand the human response to digital and physical advertisements. They sent out 1,950 invitations to assess the interest of potential candidates in a popular graduate program in a major US university. Participants were split into four groups: physical print only (PP), digital/email only (DD), physical then digital (PD), digital then physical (DP). Each participant was sent the same advertisement twice, one week apart, in either physical or digital email form. In the digital view, participants were asked to click on a link to receive more information. In the physical view participants were given a URL and a QR code to scan.

Condition	Group 1 (PD)	Group 2 (DP)	Group 3 (PP)	Group 4 (DD)
Total media received	497	499	482	491
Media open rate	69.82%	70.54%	N/A	65.14%
URL clicks	2.51	3.98	0.6	3.25
Applicants	6	5	2	1

Table 3: Results of study into print versus digital marketing

The results showed that the multimode sequences strongly outperformed the single-mode sequences. The number of applicants, which was the bottom line for this campaign, was significantly higher for the multimode campaigns, totalling 11 compared to 3 for the single mode. This showed that when print is included in the media channel mix of a campaign, it multiplies the traffic of any other media included in the mix.

Interestingly, participants also indicated they would pay more for items shown in a mixed-media sequence. This finding suggests that presenting products in mixed media or multichannel campaigns could allow marketers to try for higher selling prices, or that this channel may be particularly useful when marketing a product with a high ticket price.

Canada Post traffic multiplier

In 2016, Canada Post sponsored a neuroscience study[4] into the way participants consciously and unconsciously interact with various advertising media. They used the most advanced neurophysiological (EEG and eye-tracking) techniques, along with traditional surveys. This approach allowed them to examine the conscious and unconscious responses of the participants to the advertising media presented.

EEG recordings allowed researchers to assess each participant's emotional response to the advertisements. Eye-tracking helped interpret the EEG(brain activity) data by showing how long and at which moment each participant's attention was captured by particular stimuli.

Every participant was exposed to two types of media for each of the two advertising campaigns tested. Their physiological measurements were taken unobtrusively as they interacted with each medium. This was followed the next day by an online survey.

The researchers found printed media held participant attention for 118% longer, and stimulated a 29% higher brand recall than display advertising. Offer recall from print was 39% higher than for display.

A key finding of the study was the power of multichannel marketing campaigns. Those that integrated print with other media generated more attention, emotional involvement and brand recall than solely digital campaigns.

Integrated digital and direct-mail campaigns elicited 39% more attention than single-media campaigns. This effect peaked when print followed email, outperforming the average for every other combination by 40%.

Force multiplier

The US Postal Service (USPS) conducted a neuromarketing study[41] into cross-modal marketing, looking at ad sequencing using digital channels and physical prints. They conducted two and three-step campaigns, both in the field and the laboratory. In the field experiments, they recorded response rates throughout the campaign. In the lab, they collected self-reported responses to questions and recorded neurological responses to the ads. They found the cross-modal campaigns that included print generated a response rate 300% higher than the unimodal campaigns.

The influence of print does not stop once it gets people into the store. Print is a critical sales tool at the moment of purchase. When the customer is on the verge of making a purchase and they want to really drill down on the details and understand what they are buying, they want to read it on paper. It was consistently found across multiple industries that customers relied on print to help make the final decision to purchase.

A Roy Morgan survey asked Australians to rank the media most useful when making purchasing decisions[42]. Catalogues ranked first across 11 categories, second across 4 categories and third across 2 categories. The highest rankings were groceries at 52%, children's wear and toys at 44%, alcoholic beverages at 43% and small electrical appliances at 41%.[43]

Brand Science conducted a study into the effect of executing a print and internet marketing campaign . They found that a typical online campaign will pay back 62% more and the TV component pays back 37% more when there is direct mail in the marketing mix[44]. That is a significant increase in the results of any marketing campaign.

People like digitally integrated print

In a large 2013 focus group study of digital natives[45], the USPS found that young consumers responded well to digital integration with QR codes. The ability to instantly obtain more information about a product through digital features especially impressed participants in the study.

> *Everything is digital. We should not separate, we should integrate.*
>
> — Roel de Vries (Nissan CMO)

Specifically, they found mail pieces with digital features more informative, efficient and useful than mail pieces without them. The younger audience appreciated that the business recognised their fondness for researching products and completing trans-actions online.

Digital natives said they would value printed messages even more if the technology integrated into mail pieces was easy to use. The quality of the mail piece and any interactive feature it provided was especially important to the focus group participants.

This study was specifically targeted at a younger demographic but I believe the findings are relevant to everyone. In a way, we are all digital natives. The case study at the end of Chapter 5 is about the Salvation Army campaigning for donations. They used an omni channel campaign, employing every advertising channel available, and actively worked to track as much of the activity as possible to accurately attribute it to allow for fine-tuning in following campaigns. One of the things they found was the overwhelming majority of donations were made online. This behaviour was consistent across all demographics.

Every demographic uses screens – they make a lot of things easy. We are all digital natives to some degree, so we all like print that has digital features.

Screens

When it comes to internet marketing, it is useful to consider screens, for example the smartphone or computer, as a single channel rather than multiple channels. While it's true that YouTube is separate from Twitter, which is separate from Facebook and so on, users experience them all in the same way. Through a device, the human interface is the same. We are holding our phone and looking down at it or sitting at our desk looking at the screen.

Exacerbating this further is the way the internet giants work so hard to keep showing users the same kind of content. If you interact with an ad on Facebook, or search a term on Google, that content will follow you around the internet in search results and on banner ads on websites. If you search something on YouTube, the algorithm will start feeding you more and more content in that subject field. Open Netflix with another person's login and you will be presented with viewing suggestions completely different to what you would see via your login. All of this has made the internet a homogenised experience that will never surprise us and is always the same, no matter what platform we use.

Bhaskar Chakravorti of Tufts University studied[46] trust in digital technology and how it affects user behaviour. In areas of the world with smaller digital economies and where technology use was still growing, Chakravorti found users tend to stick with a website, even if it loads slowly, is hard to use or requires many steps to make an online purchase. This could be because the experience is still novel and there are fewer convenient alternatives, either online or offline.

User behaviour is different in the mature digital markets of western Europe, North America, Japan and South Korea, where people have been using the internet for many years. Here, users are prone to switching away from sites that don't load rapidly or are hard to use, and they abandon online shopping carts if the purchase process is too complex. Users abandon transactions on screens because they are bored or distracted. A marketer's hard-won activity will evaporate because an experienced user has a poor connection and little patience.

Figure 41: It's amazing how quickly things change

This is the world in which print can induce change. It offers marketers an opportunity to do something new, providing a new way for people to see artwork away from devices and offering one-to-one communication between the brand and the customer because nothing else is needed beyond sufficient lighting. Print can present artwork in a new setting – in people's kitchens or on their desks – and will inspire them to take action by going back onto the internet or into a store. Even though we are a bit sick of screens, they are very useful and are still a primary way to navigate the internet.

Imagine a customer saw your flyer and got onto your website last night, but the internet was slow so they navigated away. Tonight, they see your flyer again, still on the bench and, reminded of the offer, hop on the website again. This is the multiplier effect.

Introducing print into the mix has the effect of priming people for a second contact and the added channel also attracts new audiences, extending the reach of the campaign. With some of the audience now seeing the campaign through more than one channel, the mixture improves returns from other channels. The Temple University study showed us that 'digital plus print' produced 5 times the number of closed sales as the 'digital plus digital' campaign.

MAIL ON DISPLAY

The display area is particularly important. In the ethnography films, we noticed how mail was used as functional decoration, occupying a designated space in a room. The quantitative follow-up survey identified that 39 per cent of people displayed mail in the home, most commonly in the kitchen, providing multiple opportunities to engage with a brand.

—Royal Mail, *The Private Life of Mail*, 2015[47]

Royal Mail's study, *The Private Life of Mail*, shows that after print that enters the home, it is likely to be on display or stored in a high-traffic area, creating multiple opportunities for the piece to have the same effect on all the household members. It is easy to see how often the residents of a household would see the piece and, if the print is an effective integration hub, it is easy to imagine how it would serve to increase traffic at other active channels.

Paper brings focus

Still point

Interacting with paper is centring for people; it 'becomes a still point, an anchor for the consciousness'[48]. One can manage a number of printed documents without becoming distracted as we do with other channels. Print provides us with an anchor from which we can venture online or to a shopping centre, only to return to be reminded of why we went in the first place.

Multiplying effect – paper focus

When people read a printed document, they can switch to another channel without losing focus. A person can sit on the couch and look through a printed catalogue and switch to their smartphone to research a specific item, and perhaps purchase it, then come back to the catalogue. The same is not true of any other channel. Phone numbers heard on radio or TV quickly evaporate from the memory. Subsequently, advertising strategies on these formats depend on multiple exposures and catchy tunes. The internet is designed to keep us distracted and staring at the screen; it wants us to forget what we were doing so we will watch more cat videos. The internet makes money by capturing our attention and keeping it and it does this by constantly presenting us with new distractions. Paper, by contrast, is steady and constant. While the internet is an everchanging feast of everything, paper is just this one thing – ready to bring our focus back to its single message.

This is the foundation of the traffic multiplier effect of print.

The online component of a typical marketing campaign pays back 62 per cent more when there is direct mail in the marketing mix[49]

—*Meta Analysis of Direct Mail* (Royal Mail, 2012)

Print is a springboard

Trusted links

Print can work well as a referral hub for other channels because it is inherently trusted by the reader. The JD Williams case study (p.107) and Temple University study (p.89) show similar results. The addition of a printed component increased the credibility of the digital and email components of the campaign, as shown in the Temple University data by the higher click-through rates. Our trust in print is deeply ingrained in our culture and is part of how we interact – a contract is confirmed by the paper it is printed on because the 'information is right here in black and white'. Recording information as ink on paper makes it more significant and trustworthy.

Imagine receiving a message claiming to be from your bank and informing you that your account had been breached and asking you to review the attached document, then contact the bank via a given phone number or URL to confirm and update your card details and security passwords. It is a high-stakes communication. Now, imagine receiving this message in two formats – one as a printed letter in the mail and the other as an email.

In the physical letter form, it arrives in a branded envelope. The letter is printed on a corporate letterhead and the attached document is a glossy, branded multipage booklet. In the digital email form, it arrives as an email with a file attachment. This email should be treated with great suspicion and care, particularly any links or attachments. Theoretically, either form could be a scam but people will trust the paper almost immediately while the email should not be trusted at all. Online fraud and identity theft are very real dangers of the internet and devalues every online communication, including legitimate ones.

Stimulating action – paper springboard

The trust we place in printed information means the connecting tools (phone numbers, URLs etc.) included on the printed item have a high chance of being acted on.

By holding the trust of the audience, printed marketing material can become a referral hub that links all the physical and virtual platforms of a brand. This makes it possible to move the customer into the digital marketing ecosystem or into direct contact with the sales department.

Finding the right balance of channels to reach increasingly fragmented audiences is the key to successful marketing strategies.

Diminishing returns

To play the devil's advocate, if the goal of a printed marketing piece is to get the audience to a website, why would you invite them to your Facebook page? Wouldn't focusing on a single goal and limiting the integration options be more effective at directing traffic?

There is a point of diminishing returns for each marketing channel when it becomes more cost-effective for the overall campaign to add a new channel, and access a new audience, rather than investing more in an existing channel in a vain attempt to extend reach. For example, the people who are going to click on your email have already done so. Sending another email is not going to get many more clicks. The people who are likely to go to your website will do so whether there is a Facebook icon on there or not. However, by excluding the Facebook icon, you will miss out on the people who prefer using Facebook.

Here is a story to illustrate this point.

A chance missed

I introduced Mike, an insurance broker, to Martina, a friend who needed life insurance. A week later, Martina told me Mike had called her a couple of times and left voicemails but due to the nature of her work, she couldn't take calls during the day. Instead, she sent Mike a text with her email address and asked him to contact her via email. A few weeks, later Mike told me he had left multiple voicemails but he was finding Martina hard to contact. I told him she couldn't take calls and he should email her. A week later, Martina said Mike had left more voicemails asking her to call back but he'd sent no emails. Eventually, Mike stopped calling. He never emailed Martina. His dogged persistence in sticking to the communication channel he preferred meant he missed the chance of making the sale.

Favourite channels

Among the many communication platforms available, we each have a favourite we use every day. You will see a message sent to you on your favourite platform but you might miss it on another platform. If you send a Facebook message to an occasional Facebook user, they might not see it for a month or they may never see it. If you call someone who won't answer their phone during the hours you are calling, you will never reach them. Conversely, when you use the right platform, for example, if you email someone who lives in their inbox, you will get a response directly. One marketer told me about a prospect he had been emailing for years with no response; he changed tactics and sent her a text and she replied right away.

Greg Portell, Lead Partner at A.T. Kearney[50], states:

Consumers don't shop in channels defined by retailers. They shop when time and interest allow, sometimes that is surfing the internet, strolling the mall, or flipping through pages in a catalogue. By moving beyond their traditional digital platforms, companies like eBay and Amazon are able to engage consumers more broadly.

It costs nothing to add a connection tool onto the graphic design, and you might gain a customer. The audience needs to interact with your content a certain number of times before they will be comfortable making a purchase. How many times will depend on the person but you should help them make those contacts as easily as possible by including all the connections available. This will make it easier for people to use their favourite channel and simultaneously expand the reach of the advertisement.

Connect the dots

Customers will swap across to the different channels using one of the common connection or integration tools or bridges.

- email address
- phone number
- street address
- QR code
- URL
- product name
- business name
- social media

Transfer to sales

The first three connections – email address, phone number and street address – all involve active contact from the customer to the brand. This is when the relationship progresses from the marketing department to the sales department. These connections are discussed in greater length in Chapter 5.

QR codes

QR codes can be included in any print communication to link users to your internet marketing ecosystem. The codes are different from a URL because they require a smartphone to make the connection. The benefit for your marketing drive is that the QR link is direct from print to phone and hence integrates sound and video with your printed collateral. All iPhones and most Android phones since 2019 have been able to read QR codes without needing an additional app.

The Covid-19 pandemic saw people 'checking in' with a QR code at every retail location. This has done a lot to normalise QR codes – everyone is familiar with them now, so usage rates are likely to be higher than previously. In a media release in March 2021, the NSW government released information about the Service NSW app that allowed people to perform the Covid-19 check in using QR codes. The app was downloaded more than 4 million times, accounting for approximately 75% of the adult population of NSW. More than 80,000 businesses were actively using the QR code check-in feature and it had been used by patrons for more than 117 million check-ins, with around 2.5 million check-ins a day.

What this means is most of the adult population is now very familiar with QR codes.

QR codes can perform the following functions:

- open a website URL
- enter contact details into a phone directory
- open a video or audio URL or a social media profile
- register an event
- download an app or a file

The codes are available online for free or you can use paid services that work better. Investing in a paid QR code service will enable you to record data, such as traffic levels, and to know where and when the code was used.

Web URLs

You can provide web URLs in a printed piece. These are internet addresses the audience can manually enter into a web browser or use to double-check they are on the right path after they search online for your business name.

A typical URL is a long, nonsensical string of letters that is very easy to mistype, creating a failure point. You can lower the risk of failure by using a URL shortener, like TinyURL, that will reduce the length of the URL to around 10 characters. There are multiple other online providers that offer this service for free, or your web developer could help you with website plugins or redirects. The paid URL shorteners offer traffic recording functions to help you measure response rates.

Product name

Any Search Engine Optimisation (SEO) you have done to position your brand online will help your marketing drive. When you promote a product, the audience will research your product name online. Ideally, when they locate the name, they will also find your website.

It is possible to create a new name for a generic product so you can own the name on search engines. A business that does this can use the name exclusively on their website. The product is the same but the business uses a different name for it. In this way, the business has created a valuable niche for themselves at little cost. When customers search for that product name, the business website comes up.

This is not a new idea, a well know example is McDonalds. They give all of their burgers a unique name like Big Mac. The Big Mac is still a burger, but is a uniquely McDonalds burger.

This idea is founded on the effective use of SEO so you would be well advised to discuss it with an expert in that field. Ranking high in organic search engine results is effective if you can harness it. It has been said that the best place to hide a body is on the second page of Google search results.

Business name

Interested people will search your business name online, if only as a way of finding your website. Your business name is one of the most important elements of the graphic design – make sure it is clearly visible and easily read.

Including the business name in marketing collateral seems obvious but leaving it off marketing collateral is not uncommon, particularly with small businesses and trades. A marketer might choose to call the business 'Your Local Electrician', or other trade, hoping to take advantage of people preferring to work with local trades. Not including the business name will create mistrust in your business and will reduce the effectiveness of the campaign.

Social media

Because around 80% of businesses have a Facebook page, including the logo seems unnecessary but it will cost you nothing and could convert more sales. Including all the social media logos is an easy way to tell customers you can be found on those platforms. One social media expert described a social media search of a business as akin to a basic health check. It's a quick way for the customer to get a feel for the brand.

Examples

Combining print and online content is an exciting new space for marketers to move into, and it is not seen often. It is hard to explain but easy to show, so I have compiled a few interesting examples for inspiration and food for thought.

Augmented reality

Augmented reality (AR) is a new technology that was boosted by the worldwide sensation of the video game, *Pokémon Go*. The game saw people wandering the streets, peering at their surroundings through their smart phone and hunting monsters that were only visible on their screen. This technology is available to marketers. I encountered this in a botanical garden as a dinosaur display. Information displays featured QR codes that triggered a screen overlay of dinosaurs walking among plants and people in the park. The program made a lasting impression on my children who, years later, still refer to the gardens as the dinosaur park.

Around 66% of people say they are interested in using AR for help when shopping.

—Google Consumer Augmented Reality Survey,
Global, 2019[51]

Software companies such as Viewa and Zappar use AR through their free app on your smartphone, which scans the printed page. The technology can bring a model in a photo to life in your camera, have a spokesperson appear to stand on the printed page, offer games of skill or present chances to win prizes.

AR can convert a wall graphic on a store window from a static image to a full action video when viewed through the AR app on a smartphone. This can be done with any image. For example, a surfer in a still photo could start surfing the wave in a moving image. It is a new and growing field that fosters exceptionally close connections between audience and brand.

Digital then print – springboard

It is possible to make the first connection through the internet and then a following connection through print, continuing the conversation with the customer through the longer dwell time and the information retention possible with print.

There is an opportunity to connect first with digital and then push to the longer dialogue through print media, with print's longer dwell time and, therefore, strong message and brand recall.

UK online retailer, JD Williams, was seeking to reduce their level of abandoned carts. Traditionally, they followed up abandoned carts with two emails that showed images of the items from the abandoned cart. In an effort to lower this level, they ran a split test. The first group received 3 follow-ups, the second group received 2 and the third communication was a printed follow-up. The printed item used similar artwork and imagery as in the emails. For the group who received the print, response rates increased by 6%. Average order value increased by 8%. Abandoned cart rates were reduced by 14%.[52]

On the page integration

The proliferation of smartphones has made possible another approach to connecting readers with online content by integrating digital content onto the printed page.

Video integration

Another option is integrating video with graphic design on the printed page through a smartphone screen. The design should include a printed frame, about the size of a smartphone, to show the audience where to place the phone when the video plays. With the phone on the page and the video playing, the effect resembles the animated newspapers from the Harry Potter movies.

When promoting the new Ford Explorer, BBR Saatchi & Saatchi Israel created a series of 3 print ads that brought visual demonstrations of the vehicle's key features to life through the reader's smartphone. A QR code linked through to a video and the reader then placed their phone on the printed page, animating it.

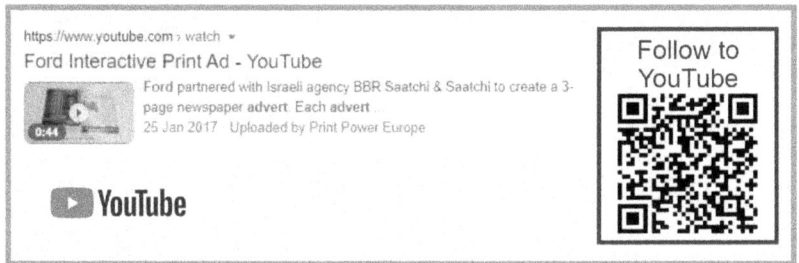

Figure 42: Animated print Ford Explorer ad

Figure 43: Scan the QR code to see the animated Ford Explorer ad in action

'Reporters Without Borders' took a similar approach. Their print ads featured full page portraits of 3 dictatorial world leaders, with a frame for the phone over their mouth. A QR code in the corner loaded a film of a mouth, not the dictator's but a journalist's, which began talking about the dangers of being a reporter in that country.

Figure 44: Reporters Without Borders print ads utilised QR codes for impact

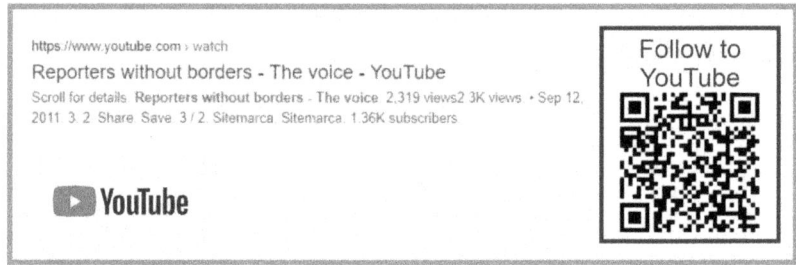

Figure 45: Scan the QR code to watch the Reporters Without Borders ad

Lexus took on the same idea, developing an approach they called CinePrint. This time, the video played under the paper with the light of the screen showing through. The Lexus ad required the reader to use an iPad to navigate to a video, which was placed under the print ad to play the video. The screen illuminated the ad from beneath and the previously static ad became a moving car with different backgrounds and music on the printed page.

Figure 46: CinePrint ad developed by Lexus

Figure 47: Scan the QR code to view the Lexus ad

Best practice

The 2013 USPS study, *Enhancing Mail for Digital Natives*[53], found icons or universally used logos, like social media or QR codes, are more effective than simple black and white text to let the reader know what connections are available. Text-only instructions were often missed or skipped, while recognisable icons were seen and acted on by more readers.

Participants stated that the print graphic design must include a clear message that the printed piece contained a digital feature. The study emphasised the need for the design to prominently feature instructions on how to use the digital component.

Some simple guidelines to consider when designing the artwork include:

- **Use third party logos**
  These are a visual shorthand for the link destinations. For example, everyone knows a Facebook icon means the business is on Facebook. Use the public profile of the tech giants to your advantage and let people know quickly where you want them to go and what to expect, by using their logos.

- **Use recognisable icons**
  Communicate quickly what you want people to do. The phone icon or a download icon are simple pictograms packed full of meaning and are an easy way to clearly communicate your intention. They aren't sexy, but they are functional.

Figure 48: Simple, recognisable icons

- **Make it noticeable**

  Make the digital components and offline connections colourful and noticeable. People want to go online so make it easy for them to notice the online option. The URL for your webstore shouldn't be tucked away with the terms and conditions. Print is a springboard and a traffic multiplier so make those links obvious and let your print launch people onto your internet ecosystem.

- **Provide clear instructions**

  Clearly state there is an online feature and provide a brief overview of what people need to do. This is particularly applicable to QR codes, which could do anything. Communicate what the QR code will do in simple language.

- **Shorten the URL**

  Use URL shorteners. A long URL is hard to remember and easy to mistype. URL shorteners are easy to set up and have the additional benefit of allowing for traffic measurement, which will help attribute activity to the printed piece.

Case study

Links from paper to sound

Kontor Records in the UK wanted to promote a new artist to London recording agencies. Persuading recording agency people to listen to a new artist is particularly difficult. They receive demonstration tracks every day and many of those go straight into the bin. To cut through, Kontor developed a remarkable mail-out solution. Using digital printing with digital profile cutting and scoring techniques, they created a large envelope that contained a paper LP record. The envelope itself was scored and cut so it folded from an envelope into a paper LP record player. Using a QR code printed on the paper LP player, the recipient opened an online media player with their smartphone, which they placed on the indicated spot on the paper LP player. An animation played on their phone, showing a needle and a rotating LP record while playing the music the talent agency was promoting. At the end of the track, the audience was prompted to navigate into a music library with access to more of the talent agency's list of artists. It was a remarkable solution that headlined a specific artist and promoted the rest of the talent agency's clients at the same time. Some 75% of recipients opened the LP player app and a further 60% explored the talent agency's music library.

Figure 49: Scan the QR code to see how Kontor Records got their clients noticed

Figure 50: Kontor Records paper record player

Key points in Chapter 4

- A printed item becomes a hub for other media, expanding the power of the message.
- Use of several channels, particularly online, creates a multiplier effect for your marketing.
- University tests have shown that multi-mode messages outperform those in a single medium, on every measure.
- Use print as part of a multimedia integrated mix.
- Use print to point people towards online content. The time of mail order catalogues is over. People can complete purchases online so use print to get them there.

Chapter 5
Preparation – prepare the way

Gains from well-planned marketing

The customer journey begins when the customer first encounters a marketing campaign and finishes at the point of purchase. Between the first contact and the purchase, there will be many potential points of contact between a customer and the brand. They may go from a flyer to Instagram, to Facebook, to an email, then to an instore purchase. All roads lead to Rome in the end but it's not a linear funnel.

Many of those contact points will be online. In recognising this fact, marketing campaigns should be multichannel and use print to direct traffic to online content, moving the customer towards the point of purchase.

Print is a shotgun with great capacity to generate downstream traffic into all online and offline points of contact for a brand but there is no automation to lean on – it's all manual. To get the most out of print, the marketer must prepare all of those downstream points of contact to accommodate the activity generated by print.

Just like marketers had to do 30 years ago, the modern marketer must prepare the rest of the business because no one else is doing it for them.

Losing warm leads

Susan is a finance broker who writes many business loans; she has decades of experience and many customers. An industry lender sent her a high-quality, well-produced A4 booklet of 16 pages, full colour on heavy gloss stock and incorporating professional graphic design and copywriting. The printed piece communicated uniformly positive messages about their brand. Susan was impressed. She hopped on their website and found a landing page about the promotion but couldn't find the exact product from the booklet on the main website. She had a few questions about the specific products and has always found it easier to talk to someone, so she rang the number on the brochure. The receptionist wasn't sure what brochure Susan was talking about but took a message. Susan waited a couple of days and, after hearing nothing, rang again. This time, she was transferred to a sales rep's answering machine, where she left another message. They never got back to her and she never called them again.

Susan was the perfect customer for the lender – a sophisticated operator with a high potential lifetime value to the lender's business. Attracting a customer like Susan is the exact reason the lender's marketing team ran this campaign, but they lost her because the marketing team did not fully prepare the rest of the business to accommodate the increase in activity.

Unfortunately, the marketer thought their job finished with producing and distributing the brochure. They did nothing to prepare the website or to prepare the sales team to handle or record Susan's enquiry. Reception did not know why she was calling, nor did they know who to pass her on to. No record was taken of her call, meaning no one followed up with Susan.

The lender invested in high-quality print production and graphic design. It was the quality of the printed piece that motivated Susan to act, but the lack of preparation made the campaign fail. With no data recording the activity produced by the printed piece, and doubtless plenty of data from the online campaign elements, the marketing team likely concluded that the print medium failed – not that they had only done half their job.

Map the journey to the customer

The channels for connection are more numerous than in the past but they are finite. Take an aerial view of how a customer might move through a marketing ecosystem and map each marketing element. There are only six ways that a customer may contact the brand:

1. Visit your website
2. Send you an email
3. Give you a call
4. Search on social media
5. Visit your shop
6. Research you or your product online

Make sure each way is prepared in advance.

Next actions

Consider a 2017 study by research group, JICMAIL[54], which used a rotating panel of over 1000 households a month that completed a diary-based app in which they captured an image of every mail item they receive in a week. The app recorded what type of mail it was and who sent it, and then recorded exactly what they did with the item, both immediately and over a 28-day period. They found participants would perform one of the following commercial actions:

- Visit the company's website
- Buy something
- Make a donation
- Plan a large purchase
- Use a voucher or code
- Visit the company's shop
- Order a catalogue
- Tell others about an offer

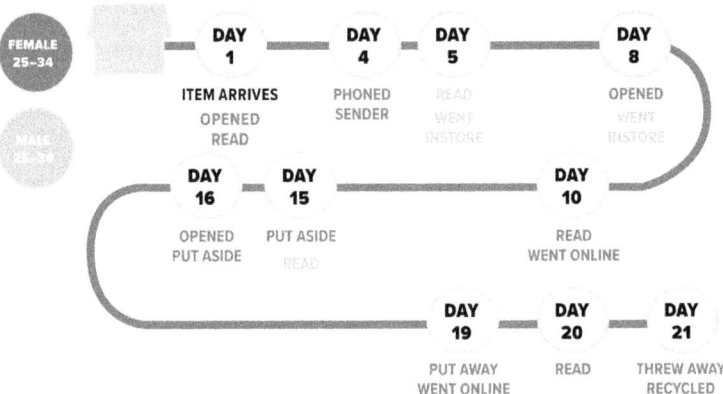

Figure 51: What happens with our mail?

The example below tracks mail landing in a household with two adults under 35 and a child. Here, we can see the mail item was revisited several times by both adults and generated multiple actions, including going online, making a purchase, going instore and contacting the sender.

Print will initiate a wide range of online and offline activities. The marketer needs to anticipate them all and prepare for them.

The campaign must be multichannel to accommodate the full range of possible customer responses.

It is important to note that all the activity filters down to a handful of key points that need to be prepared. The marketer just needs to identify those key points and focus their efforts there. To take Susan's case study, the mistakes made included:

- no activity tracking
- no links on the homepage to the landing page
- no preparation of the sales team.

This is not a huge number of holes and could be easily addressed

Three elements

In preparing a business there are three elements to work on.

1. **Data**

   Data needs to be collected. Print doesn't come with inbuilt data tracking like internet marketing, or a dedicated sales and research team like TV, radio or magazines. The task of attributing downstream activity generated by print falls to the marketer. If they don't, the only tracking data will come from online sources and will not attribute anything to print. This leads to incomplete data, which leads to poor decision-making in future campaigns.

2. **Offline connections**

   Sales teams need to be prepared to accommodate new activity. This means salespeople need scripts, email auto-responders need to be set up, shopfronts need signage, centre management needs posters, the car yard needs new balloons and so on.

3. Online connections

Websites and social media presences must be prepared. Print is a springboard into online marketing. Any digital connections on the print artwork must be prepared and be congruent with what the print offers.

Data

Measure activity

A survey of 192 senior-level marketers in the United States found that 48% rated their ability to measure the effectiveness of print marketing as 'fair' or 'poor'[55] – which probably means those 48% don't do print because it doesn't seem entirely necessary.

This is a mistake.

The internet is often the point of purchase and it is also rich in activity tracking. Because of this, all the data collected will be biased heavily towards internet marketing as the source of the activity. Google research says that 90% of shoppers use more than one device or platform when making a purchase[56]. Google tracking cookies can't tell you that a customer went from the printed flyer, to Google, to your website, back to the flyer, to your Instagram and then switched devices to their desktop computer to finalise the sale. The online data only reports on the online activity. The online channels are blind to the influence of print, therefore providing an incomplete understanding of the performance of campaign elements. Incomplete data puts marketers at risk of poor decisions about where to invest their budget in future campaigns.

Mail definitely positively impacted the campaign. We had feedback from sales that there were strong results from those people we called who had received the letter.

— Sam Parker, SME Marketing Manager,
AXA PPP Healthcare[57]

Incomplete data

Building a print marketing tracking system is an additional challenge for marketers but it should not be skipped. Writing about cross-channel marketing, marketing expert, Steve Olenski, said:

> *... successful marketers are nearly 35 times more likely to use cross-channel marketing with their customers versus underperforming teams who struggle to use this tactic at all. ...*
>
> *The CMO Club revealed that 82% of Chief Marketing Officers (CMOs) stated the reason they can't implement an effective cross-channel marketing strategy is because of their ability, or lack thereof, to measure it in the first place.[58]*

From what Olenski says, it can be inferred that 18% of marketers are the successful ones who can measure the influence of print within a cross-channel campaign. Print is among the most expensive marketing channels per exposure, so it is often the first to be cut to reduce spends. This is a decision made easier, at the marketer's risk, if they are relying on data like last-click attribution, which skews heavily towards online sources. With the success of future campaigns at risk, marketers need complete data to inform their choice of media channels.

In *A Bias for Action* (Canada Post, 2015), the following point is made:

> *Shoppers are moving fluidly across on[line] and offline channels throughout the purchase journey – using information gathered in one to inform decisions in the other – and brands are finding that business success increases significantly when these two worlds connect and feed each other seamlessly.*

The long tail of print

Print marketing can exist for a long time in a customer's world before they act on it. So it's best to track the effect of print campaigns on business activity for a few months after the end of the campaign.

An extensive 2015 Royal Mail study[59] into the lifecycle of mail put surveillance cameras into 12 households to see how they managed print marketing items that entered the house. This was backed up with 14 focus groups, 99 in-depth interviews, 213 participants within a neuroscience and tactility study and 9504 telephone and online surveys. They found that print was kept for an average of 38 days for advertising, 45 days for bills and statements and 60 days for catalogues. During this time, the print is typically kept on display. Of households surveyed, 39% had a dedicated area for the display of printed items.

Adding to this already long tail, Google's market research arm found that while everything else seems to be speeding up, the purchasing journey in general is slowing down. In 2019, people took 9 days longer on average to make purchase decisions when compared with 2015[60].

Key metrics

Choosing which metrics to record is an important decision because it will create the context for your decision-making. Printed material can have a long life in a customer's home and, accordingly, responses to a print campaign will span a longer period than any other channel. Continue tracking activity for 30 to 60 days after the last print distribution date, particularly with a mail-out campaign.

Below are some more suggestions for metrics or Key Performance Indicators (KPIs) to monitor the performance of a marketing campaign.

The Basics: record contact details, the nature of the enquiry and how they found you – with the basics, you can't go wrong.

Return on investment (ROI): determining ROI is a simple calculation – take the total revenue generated over a period, minus the cost of the campaign, and divide this by the cost of the campaign to work out the return on every dollar spent (i.e. $2 return for every $1 spent). ROI is a useful quick check but should not be relied on alone. ROI can be easily increased by simply decreasing expenditure, which may not be in the interest of creating growth. ROI should always be viewed in the context of other KPIs.

Sales revenue: another measure of marketing success is total revenue over a certain period of time after your campaign.

New customer acquisition: divide total marketing expenditure by the number of new customers to calculate new customer acquisition. This is a metric in which the print medium can excel. Although print is often the most expensive channel for each new contact achieved, the cost of print per new customer is often the lowest of any medium.

Customer value: customers can be assigned a possible lifetime value. Assess and categorise new customers and measure how many of each category have been acquired. A customer's potential lifetime value can make spending on print easy to justify.

Online activity: review online activity for increases before, during and after the print campaign. Check search engine activity for relevant search terms. Check website activity on your site and sites promoted through print.

Social media: check for increases in visits to social media sites and monitor likes, comments and shares.

Customer category: review which customer categories are responding and how.

Purchase size per customer category: review the purchases or cart of each customer category.

Product per customer category: review product sales to each customer category.

Customer preferences: monitor response rates for different calls-to-action on email, phone and online. Check the spread of responses and the peak, and review the steps customers take from response to placing an order.

Other key factors: take account of the effect of external factors, such as the weather and the timing of delivery by day, week, month and year.

Measurement: Ways to assess the power of print

Below are some suggestions for ways to measure the effectiveness of print.

Customer surveys: ask customers how they found you. Provide a list the channels used in the campaign and ask them to choose the top three that influenced them.

Phone feedback: when you have customers on the phone, take the opportunity to ask them questions similar to the survey above.

Follow-up calls: about a week after supplying a customer, call and ask how your business performed. You will get some constructive feedback and if something has gone wrong, it can be fixed it before they complain or write a negative review. In this way, you can turn a negative into a positive.

Offer codes or coupons: put a special offer on a flyer or coupon to be used online or over the counter. This will identify the source of activity. Big companies, such as Domino's Pizza, do this regularly, sending customers from a printed flyer to buy online.

Offline connections

Reverse showrooming

In 2015, PricewaterhouseCoopers (PwC) conducted a global consumer survey[61] with over 19,000 respondents in 19 territories on 6 continents. They were researching the changing retail environment in our post-digital age. One of the surprising findings was what they called 'reverse showrooming' behaviour. Customers in the recent past often visited a retail store to assess a product, then purchased the item online. The PwC survey, however, found this behaviour had reversed. The trend they identified was towards customers researching an item online then buying from a shop. PwC found that increases in online traffic were fostering instore sales and, conversely, that offline channels, such as print, were effective in sending traffic to online sites.

83% of US shoppers who visited a store in the last week say they used online search before going into a store.

– Think with Google[62]

This shows us that while communication methods have changed with the smartphone and internet, people haven't changed. They still like going to the shops. Some of the details have changed but it is still the same essential behaviour as it was before the internet. So 'traditional' offline connections are still important. The marketer must anticipate offline responses through email, phone and foot traffic. The sales team, and bricks and mortar stores, must be included in the marketing campaign to keep the customers' journey consistent.

The transfer

The three connection bridges – email, phone and street address – are the points when a customer transfers from the marketing ecosystem into sales and other normal operations of the business. Marketers cannot afford to assume that normal operations will automatically pick up enquiries generated by their campaign. An unprepared transfer is a potential mishap that can leave the sales team flat-footed as warm leads slip through their fingers. Carefully consider what instore signage, email address, phone number and street address is used, and how to record activity at those points of contact. Email responses, call scripts and activity recording processes must be implemented at the transfer stage. Good preparation at this stage will allow you to measure the success of the campaign and aid your success by finding and closing any gaps through which leads might escape.

Prepare sales departments so they know what to expect, work with them to create phone scripts, email responses and procedures with which to respond to enquiries. Most importantly, provide them with ways to record the source of inquiries. All of this must have built-in ways to identify offline sources of activity.

This doesn't have to be complicated, and doesn't require a subscription to Salesforce. It can be done with a simple spreadsheet on a shared drive, an email template to send in response, an internal contact to pass the call onto, or an internal email address to send the contact details to for follow-up. These are all simple steps that will increase the effectiveness of the campaign.

Training resources

Create training resources about how to use the record-taking system. Loom is a free screen and webcam recording tool that only requires a webcam and a browser to use. You can record yourself explaining and demonstrating, on-screen, how to use the record system as though the person is sitting next to you. Loom will give you a link you can email to colleagues and, as easy as that, you have created a procedure and trained everyone how to use your record system. This will create a robust system that isn't dependent on any single person to keep operating. It will allow you to track performance, identify failure points and so improve performance on future campaigns.

Email address

When deciding which email address to use for a campaign, consider creating a new email address, dedicated to the campaign. This is simple and can often be done without cost. A specific email address for a marketing purpose will help you control responses and track enquiries.

Set up an auto-responder for any incoming mail addressed to the dedicated email address, then forward messages to the appropriate email address in the sales department. Tracking activity can be done through a simple search for all messages sent to that email address, which will count the email activity.

Without upsetting any pre-existing email set-ups, the campaign has a simple and automated system that sends a scripted reply to the email enquiry, forwards it to the appropriate team member and tracks activity in the system.

Another option is direct enquiries to a generic or existing email address. The goal is to decide which email address will be promoted in the campaign and have a procedure ready to respond to the enquiry and record the activity.

Phone number

Specify the phone number that respondents will call, whether it is a mobile number or a landline, and whether to send the calls to head office or to a virtual receptionist or call centre. These decisions are significant, as is tracking activity and attributing the activity to its source.

Street address

If the campaign drives customers to visit a location and not a website, it's obviously important to include the street address. If there are multiple addresses, specify which one people should visit.

If a prospective customer has too much trouble getting to the location, they will not enter and buy. A common mistake is including the minimum of information regarding addresses. Make it easier for people to visit by adding a more information about the location, where the best place is to park or a small map that shows major roads and the store location.

It can be said that the carpark is the first step in your sales process. Firstly, make sure people can get there. Secondly, make sure there is signage consistent with any active campaign and it makes it clear to customers which door they need to enter.

If there's a staff member they should talk to, include the name: 'Ask for John' or 'Show this flyer' can foster confidence to come in and visit your business and it can give you a mechanism for tracking activity.

Online connections

There are a lot of opportunities to connect readers to an online content catalogue discussed earlier in this book. The marketer has to ensure that when they try to connect from the print to an online asset, they aren't left with a dead end.

Consider the following categories of online media that you are deploying in the campaign and which are pre-existing, as well as where a person might end up and how you might get them towards content about your promotion.

- Social media
- Landing page
- Home page
- Email outreach
- Video

Aim all of the digital content at a single point that can operate as a hub for all the other content. The home page is a good place to work as a hub, as it will be the easiest to find from a web search. Susan's experience showed us that a landing page that can't be easily found from the home page is a problem.

If possible, all activity, from print to online assets, should be tracked. This can be done through QR codes, URL shorteners or specific URLs that are only listed on print artwork. People may not use any of these tools and may access your home page via a search engine, though prompted by print. A good catch-all would be a questionnaire during the sales process, or as part of a sales follow-up, to ask them what media channel prompted them to go to your website.

Email outreach

Timing of emails to arrive in sequence with a printed mail-out will significantly increase response rates and the perceived value of a product. I have read multiple studies on sequencing and there is no correlation between them regarding which is better to receive first, print or email. However, there is agreement that a combination of both is better than a unimodal campaign. From my experience it can be difficult to judge delivery times precisely particularly for nationwide mail-outs, which makes worrying about which arrives first moot. Best practice is to use both channels, but I wouldn't worry too much about the order they arrive in, just that they arrive within a few days of each other.

Case study

The Salvation Army's marketing prowess

The Salvation Army worked with advertising agency, Mike Colling & Company (MC&C) from 2007 to 2012. By carefully tracking the marketing activity and the customer response to it, they were able to accurately attribute the results to each channel. They built their understanding of the role each channel played in the media mix and were thus able to adjust their approach and their spending. The insights led them to increase the use of print between 2007 to 2012, increasing volume in mail (2.7x) and door drops (1.6x). Through this process MC&C increased their client's net income and profitability[63].

The original campaign: from 1987 to 2007, the Salvation Army relied on a 6-week burst of activity before Christmas to recruit new donors. They used only print media – mail, door drops, press and inserts.

The first changes: in 2008 and 2009, they started to test a different model, adding broadcast and digital media to the marketing mix. Broadcast was designed to increase the reach and digital was used to provide additional response. In both years, they recruited more donors.

The charity also received a greater response from mail and door drops, following years of decline.

Structured insight: in 4 years, by 2010, the Salvation Army's online income had quadrupled. Their modest investment in online marketing could not account for the increase.

To correctly attribute digital donations to the offline channels they travelled through, the charity established data tracking systems.

They found that mail-outs, together with television campaigns, were combining to stimulate the online response. It was a practical illustration of the multichannel multiplier effect that occurs when print is included in the marketing mix. Print primes people to engage with other media channels and retained printed items help keep donors focused and motivated on their intention to act when they switch between channels. In this case, it was often the online activity that was the final step of the marketing process.

Identifying the value of mail-outs and door drops gave the Salvation Army confidence to invest about one million pounds more in mail and television campaigns. In 2011, with their new approach, the total of new donors and net income reached record levels.

In the years from 2005 to 2007, the cost of donors recruited via mail rose by 20%. Between 2008 and 2012, the cost per new donor fell by 16%, while the number of new donors recruited grew from 50,000 to more than 136,000.

The MC&C agency attributed this extraordinary improvement in results to the 6 key lessons, outlined below. The most important is the integration between mail, broadcast media and internet.

Lesson 1: multimedia channel multiplier effect

Television amplifies the response to mail and door drops and all 3 move people online. This supports the multimedia multiplier effect when mail is included. The customer will go through multiple channels before they buy or donate. Each responder will resonate with their favourite channel and each fresh exposure to your campaign on a new channel increases the chance they will take further steps towards buying or donating.

Figure 52: Salvation Army print marketing range

DOOR DROPS FOR REACH; COLD MAIL FOR PRECISION

Door drops mop up response; addressed mail finds new donors

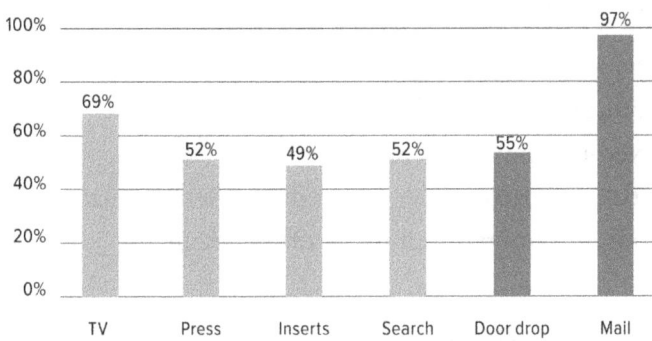

Figure 53: Analysis of Salvation Army campaign

Figure 35 shows the percentage of new donors recruited by each media channel. Door drops, with a reach of 37% of UK households in 2012, were seen by current donors and new donors; only 55% of donors recruited by the channel were new. The donors recruited by targeted mail (97%) were almost entirely new to the organisation.

Lesson 2: data collection to attribute traffic

For the Salvation Army, mail, particularly to their current donors, was a key contributor in generating most of their online income. Interestingly, even donors in their sixties chose to give online rather than by post or telephone.

If response had been measured by simple linear attribution (especially by last-click attribution), £900,000 of The Salvation Army's income in 2012 would have been allocated to digital rather than offline channels. The investment in offline media, under pressure in 2008, would not have grown without the realisation of how greatly offline marketing was contributing to online donating. Without that realisation, the Salvation Army would not have achieved such a substantial rise in their income.

Establishing data tracking systems to allow for accurate attribution is particularly important for mail. Printed items received by mail are kept in the house for days, weeks and even months. Consequently, printed marketing material draws a response for longer than many other channels.

Lesson 3: choose metrics carefully

If the Salvation Army had allocated its budget purely by year-one return on investment (ROI), they might have reconsidered using mail. Mail can struggle to perform strongly in the short term because of its high cost per contact compared with other channels. The adult cost per thousand of mail for the Salvation Army was 9 times higher than television advertising.

What produced success for the charity was the alignment of measured KPIs with marketing objectives. The primary objective for the Salvation Army was the recruitment of new donors.

Mail, although poor in year-one ROI, was the most efficient generator of response and produced the largest volume of net new donors. The individual targeting inherent in the channel meant that 97% of new donors recruited by mail were new to the organisation, compared with an average of 50% from other channels.

As a result, mail gave the best cost per new acquisition of all channels, apart from paid search (brand and advertising terms only, no generic search).

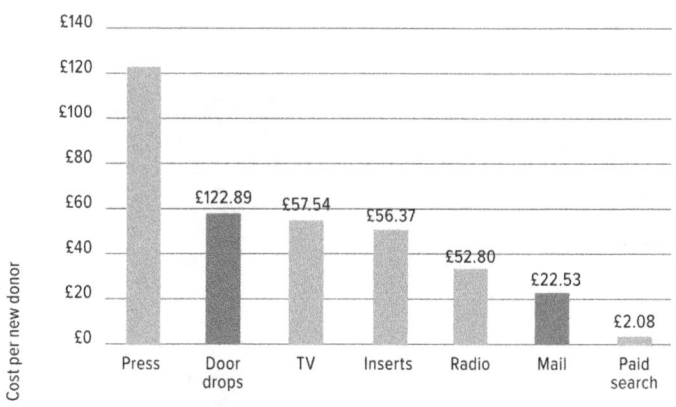

DOOR DROPS FOR REACH; COLD MAIL FOR PRECISION

Door drops mop up response; addressed mail finds new donors

Source: MC&C/The Salvation Army data, 2010

Figure 54: KPIs determine total investment totals

Had the Salvation Army allocated budget based purely on year-one ROI, they might not have achieved such a high volume of growth over 5 years. They had to sacrifice some short-term ROI over time (particularly with television) in order to dramatically increase the new donor base and achieve greater net growth in income.

The four KPIs set, agreed and measured were:

- the volume of new donors (not just donors who were prompted to give again by other channels)
- the value of each new donor over the following 5 years (this varies by channel and other advertisers might use net income over a 5-year period)
- the cost per new donor recruited
- the year-one ROI (targets set).

Figure 37 shows the result of this clarity of objectives and measurement in mail over 5 years.

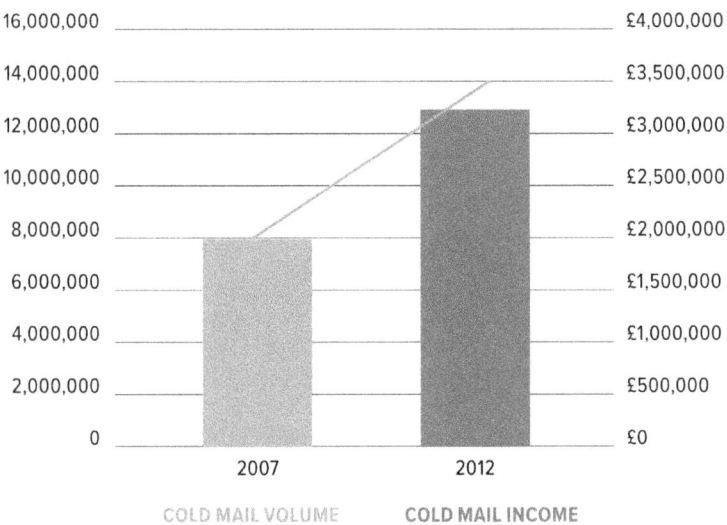

Figure 55: Volume growth in mail drove higher net income

It's worth noting that these changes were developed over 5 years, using proven direct-marketing techniques. Changes were made within a controlled test matrix, allowing a radical increase in marketing expenditure with minimal risk.

Lesson 4: tailor creative content to customer category

Not all donors are equally wealthy or as prepared to give at Christmas. The Salvation Army sent messages to new donors that were different from those sent to donors who had supported them for years.

One element of the messaging strategy is the donation prompt, or how much they ask people to give. It is a balancing act. Donors resist when they perceive the lowest nominated donation amounts to be too high. Conversely, the charity wastes an opportunity by asking too little from people who would have given more. So the Salvation Army campaign was careful to ask for a suitable amount in each donor category.

As a result, the higher value group were asked to give between £63 and £168 and achieved an average gift of £164. The lower value group were asked to give between £9 and £28 and achieved an average gift of £19.

In each case, both volume and value of response were maximised.

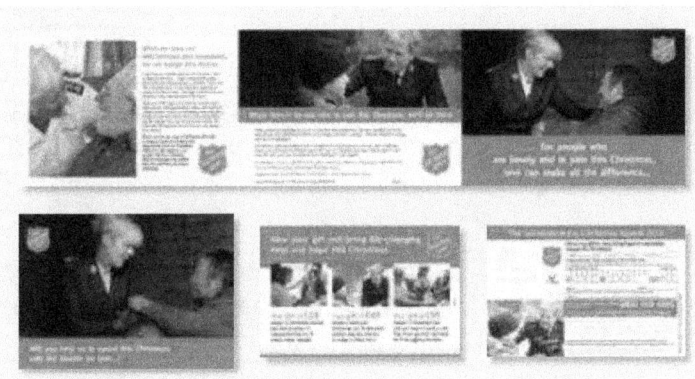

Figure 56: Samples from Salvation Army marketing campaign

Lesson 5: repeat the mail-out but not the story

The Salvation Army mailed 2 packs within 3 weeks of each other to current donors at Christmas time. By using different creative content and not merely repeating the first letter, the second pack generated an additional 40% response.

This is such an easy win for marketers using print. Deploying different design treatments within a campaign or across campaigns can increase the response rate. Something as simple as changing the colour scheme will increase results, or at least minimise any decline in response. If every flyer you send looks almost identical to the last one, people won't distinguish between the new and the old.

Lesson 6: understand how people behave with print

The Salvation Army showed genuine understanding of these principles in their award-winning work. They designed their pieces to use the strengths of print. To motivate recipients, the packaging had a headline on the outside to ensure that it was opened.

To take advantage of the fact that people spend time with print, the content featured copy with real depth to engage existing and potential donors.

Because printed items are likely to be on display for weeks, they used strong photography that allowed the pieces to be used like posters within a household, creating a mantelpiece reminder and fostering response over time.

Conclusion

Head of Marketing and Fundraising at the Salvation Army, Julius Wolff-Ingham wrote the following on the success of their marketing campaign[64]:

Mail, addressed and unaddressed, forms the absolute backbone of the Salvation Army's direct-marketing fundraising operations. It is the medium which quite literally changes lives by enabling us to raise millions of pounds in donations to fund our community and social work.

Over the last five years, we have diversified and expanded our appeals and acquisition program as new media open up. The ways in which people respond have changed too, but mail is still our anchor medium to put the Salvation Army visibly on the doormat of many millions of homes each year.

This case study reminds us of the role for mail in a modern media world. Mail, both addressed and unaddressed, has the unique capacity to generate more engagement, response and income per thousand from consumers exposed to it than any other medium.

In these days of attention scarcity that's a huge value to advertisers. When properly integrated with broadcast and digital media its benefits are amplified.

Key points in Chapter 5

- Prepare your business to track and measure the success of print media.
- Integrate all of the various elements as you progress towards a sale.
- Monitor and measure as many metrics as you can to assess financial and other returns on your marketing investment.
- Many warm leads are lost through lack of a well-planned marketing strategy.
- Track data for 30–60 days after distribution of print marketing to capture the long tail.
- A good metric to track for print marketing is New Customer Acquisition (p.125).

Chapter 6
Clarity – clear communication
Make your message work well

In the movie, *Jaws*, there is a scene in which a person at a busy beach jumps to their feet, points at the water and yells, 'SHARK!' People leap to their feet and start yelling, others start heading out of the water as fast as they can. There is no confusion, everyone understands the simple direct message: Get out of the water right now!

In directing *Jaws*, Steven Spielberg had many design decisions to make. He had to specify the sex, age and appearance of the person making the exclamation and how the shot would be framed. All of these decisions are made to enhance the central message: a person standing up and yelling 'Shark!'

Marketing artwork – the industry term for the final graphic design – is, first and foremost, a communication. For print marketing to be an effective communication, it must have a clear message that is supported by, not confused by, the later graphic design decisions.

In her classic 1955 essay on typography, *The Crystal Goblet*, Beatrice Warde equates ideas to wine and good graphic design to a crystal goblet. She points out that the finest wine glass is not wrought of solid gold but 'clear, thin as a bubble and as transparent … calculated to reveal the beautiful thing which it was meant to contain[65].' Clarity of message is paramount. Good graphic design is invisible, allowing the message to be perceived without obstruction.

Cocktail party effect

In the late 1950s, psychologist Donald Broadbent advised Britain's Royal Air Force and Royal Navy on studies of noise and technology, focusing on developing better communication between pilots and air traffic control. This focus led to the 'Filter Model of Attention' for which Broadbent is most famous. Essentially he proved a human can only pay attention to one input at a time. This is also exemplified in the 'cocktail party effect', whereby a person surrounded by talking voices can tune out all but the one they are most interested in.

The analogy Broadbent uses to explain this is a Y-shaped tube into which two flows of ping-pong balls are channelled. At the junction of the two branches of the tube, a flap acts to block one flow of balls or the other; this allows only the balls from the unblocked channel into the stem of the tube and not the balls from the other channel. Our brains operate in the same way; we tune out many of the sensory inputs we perceive.

Too much information

The cocktail party effect extends to all sensory inputs and affects the way we perceive a message within a graphic design. Too much information will result in much, or all, of the information being ignored. To create clarity in communication, it is important to strike a balance between too much information and not enough.

The Cocktail Effect
Broadbent Filter Model Attention

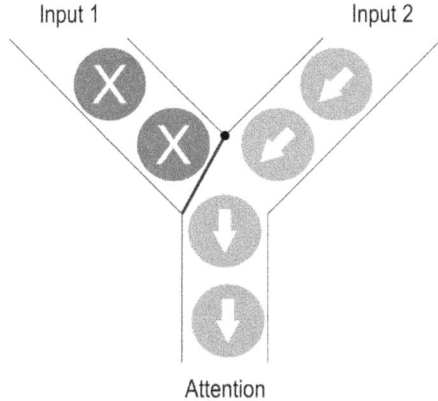

Figure 57: Donald Broadbent's model explains how our brains filter out sensory input

I saw a poster in my local grocery store that was overflowing with promotional text, images, logos and legal fine print. It was only my interest in print marketing that caused me to stand there and sift through all the information and try to sort it out. For the casual viewer, the poster was a total loss - it communicated nothing. There was a superabundance of content that obscured the core message of the piece. The whole was less than the sum of the parts.

Ronald Fernandez[66], Shopper Insight Manager of Unilever Philippines, reminds us that point of sale (POS) graphic design must fulfil 5 functions.

1. Navigation: helping users find what they need
2. Facilitation: supporting decisions on what product to buy
3. Education: teaching readers how to use a product
4. Inspiration: making shopping exciting and interactive
5. Repetition: reminding shoppers what items they forgot

Set goals

Following is a framework that will help structure your approach to developing artwork and producing consistently effective pieces of communication.

The ultimate goal

The first step is to define the ultimate goal of your marketing campaign. Most marketing campaigns are aimed at increasing sales, increasing traffic or increasing cart size. If possible, refine the goal even further, targeting a result that is specific, straight-forward and measurable.

The S.M.A.R.T goal structure is a good foundation to use:

- Specific
- Measurable
- Achievable
- Relevant
- Time-Bound

Use this structure to clearly define objectives at the outset of the campaign. They can be adjusted later.

The immediate goal

Every piece of marketing collateral has a single purpose:
to move customers to the next step, or the 'immediate goal', which will contribute to the achievement of the 'ultimate goal'. Each piece will have its own modest immediate goal. Under-standing what the immediate goal is will help shape the artwork and allow for more clarity of message.

Figure 58: Highway sign

Consider the navigation signs on the side of the highway from Sydney to Melbourne. These signs tell us when and where to turn and direct us towards the immediate goal. All the signs have their own immediate goal, such as getting drivers to take the next left, but serve the ultimate goal: getting drivers from Sydney to Melbourne.

Each element of a marketing ecosystem should operate in a similar way. For example, the immediate goal of a pop-up on a website is to get an email address. Each one will grow the email list, which will lead to greater reach for subsequent email campaigns, thus serving the ultimate goal of increasing sales.

To see how this works, look at real estate. The ultimate goal for a real estate agent is to sell a property. There are a lot of steps from the first contact between a customer and an agent to handing over the keys. The agent could attempt to short-circuit the whole process by doing a letterbox drop with a property contract and invite people to enter their financial details and sign at the bottom. They might even include a stamped self-addressed envelope so people could return the document to initiate the legal procedure of purchasing the property.

This is unlikely to work as very few people would make such an enormous decision on the spot. Obviously there is a time to bring out the contract but it's not at first contact. A better approach would be a flyer, the immediate goal of which is to get people to an open home. At the open home, another flyer has the immediate goal of getting people to contact the agent. Each asset brings the customer closer and closer to the ultimate goal.

As discussed in Chapter 5, no marketing asset should stand alone; each should support and be supported by the others. A fully-prepared campaign will be an ecosystem of marketing assets with overlapping immediate goals that work together to bring your audience towards the ultimate goal. Like a baton in a relay race, the customer should be handed from one marketing element to another.

A highway sign asks us to take the next left. It doesn't ask us to take the next left, continue for 150 kilometres and then turn right because people won't remember all of that. Each sign needs to be supported by a second sign, further down the road, that asks us to follow the next direction.

CEO of The Store in the Americas and Australasia[67], Gwen Morrison, reminds us of the following points:

- **The right message in the right place**
  Instore media is most effective when the advertised product is within reach of the customer after viewing the ad.
- **The right message at the right time**
  Throughout the week, the type of shopper could vary

depending on the day of the week and the time of day. Are the shoppers doing their regular shopping trips or just top-ups?

- **Inspire the shopper**
The content should not just be informative but also inspirational and entertaining. Shoppers who browse are typically looking for solutions, ideas and value.

The vital questions

This chapter includes quotes from successful marketers, Ronald Fernandez from Unilever, and Gwen Morrison from The Store, about how they think marketing artwork should be composed. They provide insights into the thinking of people at the top levels of marketing and visual merchandising.

Developing graphic design essentially means answering a customer's questions before they have asked them and asking them to do something. The challenge is in answering as few questions as required and not asking too much. People need to know only enough so they will do what you ask. More information than the minimum will cloud the message. By leaving information out, graphic design achieves clarity and gives certainty about granting your request. In addressing print design broadly, I believe marketing and visual merchandising artwork must answer three questions.

1. **What** is for sale?
2. **Who** is selling it?
3. **How** can they buy it?

These three questions must be answered fully and clearly or potential buyers won't buy.

This simplification does not exclude the classic 'Why?' It's a question marketers often focus on – the 'selling a lifestyle' approach. Coke ads famously work on the idea that people buy the lifestyle, not the product. I believe the 'why' is developed in copy writing, the offer and imagery, although there are better books to read about that concept.

What

Introduce the product and tell the audience about the product for sale. Clear product information will create interest and inspire people to learn more. It can, but doesn't have to be, a list of features and benefits. Or it may just be an image of the product, as with a Coke ad.

Who

Introduce the business or organisation that is offering the product for sale. Potential buyers need to know the seller because if they don't know who they are buying from, they won't buy.

If Warren Buffett, the world's greatest investor, offered advice on a stock to buy, you would probably buy it. If someone you'd never met before recommended a stock, you probably wouldn't buy it.

It is surprising how often graphic design includes little or no information about the brand supplying the service. I have seen flyers that didn't even include the brand's name. If you include affiliate logos, celebrity endorsements or quotes from reviews, these can help build confidence in the brand. At the very least, list the brand's name!

There is another aspect to consider when using print marketing. It is said the real meeting happens after the meeting. Customers will discuss and consider a proposal after the sales meeting is over. In that 'meeting after the meeting', the physical print artefact will be your only representative in the room. Elevate the reader's opinion of the brand by using high-quality paper stocks and production techniques. The approaches to create value, discussed earlier in this book, will all contribute to creating a quality printed product that will make the reader think positively about the brand. It is the equivalent of having a well-presented sales rep. A good print will better arm customers who are on board to convince those who aren't so sure.

How

The 'how' is purely functional and is a combination of the immediate goal and a connection. For example, if the immediate goal is to get the reader to call, the 'how' is the phone number –the connection. Other examples of 'how' might be 'go to this website', 'walk in this direction' or 'go to this shop'.

Use the connections that were mapped out in Chapter 4 and Chapter 5. Emphasise the connection tools for the actions you want people to take but still consider including connections for actions you don't really want taken, just to expand the reach of the advertisement. The artwork should still serve the reader and allow them to use their favourite channel.

Focus group participants talked about the fact that they valued being able to scan a catalogue that would take them to additional information about a product. Scanning a catalogue to allow for a direct purchase can make the purchase easier by taking the user directly to a web page with more information about that specific product, not the store in general.

— USPS, *Enhancing Mail for Digital Natives*[68]

Wayfinders

Wayfinders are a real-life, bare-bones example of the 3 questions being answered in a graphic design. Wayfinders are the permanent architectural signs seen hanging from the ceiling in places like shopping centres, airports and exhibition centres. They direct people to facilities such as toilets, elevators and food courts. A wayfinder is a visually simple sign that communicates a clear message. People don't generally think of them as marketing messages but they promote a service by telling people what it is, who is providing it and how to get it – answering the 3 questions.

A wayfinder will have a symbol indicating what it is directing you to – for example, an elevator, a name on a door or a toilet. It will have a directional arrow showing how to get there. It often shows the logo of the building at the bottom, telling you who is providing the service. A wayfinder might not be branded but the identity of the business is clear because it is permanently attached to the building. All 3 questions are answered with clarity.

Figure 59: Wayfinder signage in a shopping mall

Information balance

Marketing artwork must provide enough information about what is on offer and who is offering it to inspire the audience to follow clear directions about how to get there. You need to balance the right amount of information with the right kind of information.

When artwork is being developed, it is easy to add more and more design elements. The longer artwork spends in development, and the more people who have input, the more likely this is to happen. Even if it answers all 3 questions, artwork can become cluttered and cease to work as a communication.

Unbalanced artwork might provide too much information and clutter the message. It might provide too little information or the wrong information, thus defeating its purpose.

In *The Crystal Goblet*, Beatrice Ward[69] writes:

Printing demands a humility of mind, for the lack of which many of the fine arts are even now floundering in self-conscious and maudlin experiments. There is nothing simple or dull in achieving the transparent page. Vulgar ostentation is twice as easy as discipline.

To find the balance between information you need to either emphasise or minimise, print marketing can be divided into two broad categories – early contact and late contact. Understanding how the categories are used will help marketers decide what content is required to create an effective message.

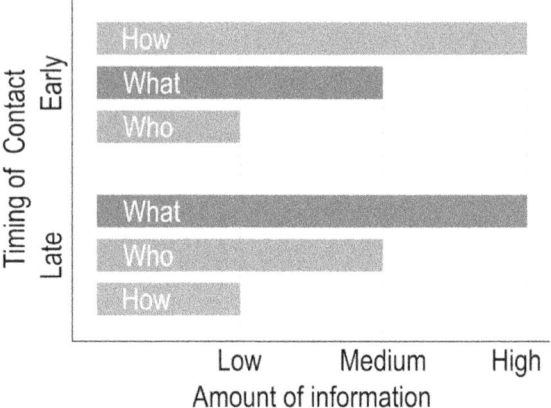

Figure 60: The balance of information is dependent on the category of contact

Category 1: early contact

The information priorities are:

1. How?
2. What?
3. Who?

Examples of early contact include wayfinders, posters, flyers, banners and building signage.

Printed items in this category are seen early in the sales funnel, with few steps before and multiple steps after, moving towards the sale operating as a referral source. Print deployed at this stage should emphasise information about how to proceed to the next stage – completing a purchase. This will be specifically aimed at the immediate goal, discussed earlier in this book, using one of the connection bridges. There should be some information about the product but it doesn't need to be comprehensive, just enough to outline the relevant features and benefits. And finally, you need just a little about the brand – the business name is probably enough.

Category 2: late contact

The information priorities are:

1. What?
2. Who?
3. How?

Examples of late contact include product brochures, menus, catalogues and booklets.

This category sits towards the end of the sales funnel, straddling the point of purchase. It is deployed just before a purchase and is referred to immediately after the purchase.

The content should focus on the product, providing a lot of information about the 'what', some about the 'who', and only a little about the 'how'. The customer may have just finalised the purchase, so the purpose is to reassure them they have made a good decision. It provides something they can sit down with and digest at their leisure to learn about their latest purchase. Alternatively, the customer is about to purchase and this will be a tool the sales team uses to direct a sales conversation or allow the customer to explore the details. Little direction is required for next steps because those directions will come from other sources, like the sales team, or from additional documents, like a contract.

Crystal goblet

Chekov's Gun

To achieve the right balance of information in the artwork, adding or removing design elements is required. Adding elements is easier than removing them because every element seems important, so it is hard to decide which can go.

There is a rule in dramatic writing known as 'Chekov's Gun', which was named for Russian author, Anton Chekhov. As a writer, you must remove everything that has no relevance to the story. If you say there is a rifle hanging on the wall in the first chapter, it absolutely must go off in the second or third chapter. If the rifle is not going to be fired, it shouldn't be hanging there.[70]

A similar approach can be used in graphic design. Assess each design element by asking:

- Does it answer the key questions of what, who and how?
- Does it add to the content or is it repetitive?
- Is the information relevant now or can it wait until later? (Less is more, especially for early contact artwork.)
- Can the entire message be understood in the appropriate viewing time?

Ruthlessly remove any element from the artwork that does not meet these criteria.

Headlines

News headlines are an example of a focused message with the singular goal of grabbing the reader's attention and encouraging them to read more. In half a dozen words or so, they summarise the article, with many details, often critical ones, left out. The ruthless exclusion of many details creates a clear communication towards the immediate goal of getting people to read the article. The full details of the story are available in the article itself. The headline doesn't need to include them all – it just needs to get people to read.

In 1984, a man entered a New York bar and shot and killed the owner. The New York Times ran the headline 'Owner of a Bar Shot to Death; Suspect is Held'. The New York Post ran the headline 'Headless Body in Topless Bar'. The Post headline demanded further reading, and quickly grabbed the attention of pop culture and even spawned a movie.

Advertising artwork is the same. Each piece does not exist in a vacuum but will be supported by the other marketing pieces that fill in the details. Each artwork just needs to get the audience to proceed to the next goal. Remember that each piece, particularly ones which are encountered early in the sales funnel, do not need to explain everything – they just have to get them interested enough to learn more; further details can be added later. In the same way, that first highway sign doesn't need to tell you about that eventual right hand turn, it just needs to tell you about taking the next left.

An effective marketing item has uncluttered artwork and a clear message. Clarity is found by focusing on less information, not more. This is emphasised by Apple founder, Steve Jobs:

People think focus means saying yes to the thing you've got to focus on. But that's not what it means at all. It means saying no to the hundred other good ideas that there are. You have to pick carefully. I'm actually as proud of the things we haven't done as the things I have done. Innovation is saying no to 1000 things.

Room to breathe

Chekov's Gun has done its job but the artwork is still cluttered.

Fashion designer, Coco Chanel, said, 'Before you leave the house, look in the mirror and take at least one thing off.' For graphic design, Chanel's advice might be to create white space around each element by shrinking design elements.

My personal graphic design practice, developed from some 20 years of experience, is to lay out the design and then shrink each element by at least 5%.

Shrinking the elements increases the white space around each one, giving them more room in which to be seen. Counter-intuitively, making all the elements smaller makes them easier to see and improves the clarity of the message.

Signages should be self-explanatory so that consumers do not require [the] assistance of the salesperson. The font type and size should be such that it is properly visible to all consumers.

—Study of visual merchandising[71]

Figure 62: Award-winning Volkswagon design from the 1960s worked as a poster and included a lot of text

Pro tips

Mail on display

If you are sending print into the house, artwork that is dense with text and information also needs to work as a poster because it will operate as a poster when pinned to a corkboard in a hallway or held to a fridge with a magnet until someone picks it up and reads it.

Print has been part of our daily life for generations and managing paper that enters the household is deeply ingrained, going into the same places in the house. Around a third of households have a specific location where printed items are stored and displayed – typically the kitchen, living room or hallway. The items can be on display for weeks to months, being viewed and shared by everyone in the house[72]. Artwork should work as a poster to attract attention, and it should also be information-dense once you have their attention.

Case study

KFC runs out of chicken

In 2018, KFC UK changed to a new freight provider to deliver chicken to their stores. A few months into the new relationship, they experienced some teething issues. Deliveries were delayed and 900 stores across the UK ran out of chicken and had to close. The official response was: The chicken crossed the road, just not to our restaurants.

We've brought a new delivery partner on board, but they've had a couple of teething problems – getting fresh chicken out to 900 restaurants across the country is pretty complex!

We won't compromise on quality, so no deliveries has meant some of our restaurants are closed, and others are operating a limited menu, or shortened hours.

The marketing team ran the artwork shown in Figure 42 in newspapers and posters and seamlessly integrated it across into the digital formats.

It was a great example of clarity of message. The empty bucket, the rearranged logo and the simple 'We're sorry'. Every element has room to breathe. The FCK alone would draw people in.

One of the challenges in designing print that will go into a home is to make a design work as a poster as well as something that carries a lot of text, to take advantage of the dwell time of print. The KFC design was an elegant example of how to achieve that. The simple bucket image at the top draws the attention, the 'we're sorry' brings you closer and then the smaller copy at the bottom gets the reader fully engaged.

Figure 61: A clear message was sent by KFC when they ran out of chicken

The five-second rule

If the message cannot be clearly perceived and understood in 5 seconds or less, it is not working. Perhaps there is too much information or not enough.

Consider the case of a billboard on the side of the road. Those couple of seconds when the audience glances at the sign is all you are ever going to get; the audience is definitely not going to turn around and pull up in front of your billboard to read the fine print.

Posters in shop windows or at shopping centres are the same. Foot traffic in a shopping centre moves constantly. People's eyes gaze around and rest on such messages for a few seconds only. Each artwork has just those few seconds to get the message across.

Even with printed items with much longer viewing times, like catalogues and menus, the five-second rule is valid. The audience flicks through the pages, scanning for information. Dense items, such as contracts and books, use headings and other editorial methods to foster quick navigation and ready understanding. Even if the artwork is full of detail, the layout as a whole needs to be coherent at a glance.

The usabilityhub.com website provides a service that allows users to fine-tune graphic designs by presenting them to other graphic designers and marketers, allowing you to ask them to complete short surveys on their impressions. This helps you maximise sales from marketing campaigns and product launches.

Viewing time

When reviewing artwork, always keep in mind the likely audience viewing time. If the audience will only spend a few seconds looking at it, review the artwork in the same time period. Can it be understood by the viewer quickly and effectively?

ABN example

The law requires certain codes to be included in the artwork. For example, a Trade Promotion / Lottery (TPL) code must be included in promotional material about a competition, and a real estate agency must display its licence number on its office door. Check the regulations for your industry. Meet the requirements, but no more. There are no bonus points for including numbers just in case.

Any superfluous content in the artwork will dilute the message. The audience's attention is finite, don't distract them with information they don't need.

The squint test

When reviewing artwork, squint your eyes as if looking at something very bright and view the artwork through your eyelashes. A clear message will be visible, even when squinting.

Stand back

During artwork development, our physical relationship with the artwork is especially close, and fixed at the distance from the face to the screen. Designers will get to a point where they can't see the forest for the trees.

Get a new perspective on the artwork. Stand up from your desk and take a step back from the screen; if there is space, walk to the other side of the room. Looking at the artwork from a distance can provide insights. Is the message is still clear?

Mr Squiggle says upside down

If the artwork isn't working, flip it on-screen and look at it upside down; the perspective will change completely. Sometimes, whatever is wrong becomes immediately apparent with this technique.

Young and old

Consider whether a 7-year-old or a 70-year-old could understand the message. If there is someone available from such age groups, ask them for their opinion with no other guidance about the question. If they can understand the message, then it's been done it right.

Case study

Apple understands the power of simplicity

Inside Apple[73], by Adam Lashinsky, provides an insider's view of one of the most influential companies of our time. Simplicity is a central value for Apple in product design and communications. When marketers walk through the front door, they walk around a light blue wall to get to their desks. On the wall, a prominent message is painted – it reads: Simplify. Simplify. Simplify.

> *If there's one thing that I take away today, and I still use, time and time again, it's that the best messaging is clear, concise and repeated.*

> —Bob Borchers, Vice-President,
> Product Marketing, Apple

The hallmarks of the Apple product message are simplicity and clarity. Throughout its history, Apple has unveiled products and features that were original or significant improvements in design and function. The simple design and strong capabilities of the first iPod and the groundbreaking multi-touch expand-and-contract feature on the iPhone were notable examples of Apple's innovative spirit.

'Apple's products are unique not only on their feature merits, but because of the way they're conceived, designed, built, sourced, manufactured, shipped, marketed, sold, opened, held and used,' says technology blogger, Charlie Kindel[5], and he is right. The simple white box, authoritative and uncluttered, that houses an Apple device quietly commands you to pick it up. It tells you only what you need to know and nothing more. The graphic design is, as Beatrice Warde would say, invisible.

Apple is incredibly consistent with the look of their marketing and packaging, creating an instantly recognisable aesthetic. Consistency of message helps build customer loyalty, and clear messaging can hugely improve profits.

Apple is so committed to creating a seamless, unobtrusive user experience that one room in their marketing building is completely dedicated to device packaging. The security here matches precautions in the sections of the building dedicated to new products and designs. At one point, before a new iPod was launched, an employee spent hours, every day for months, simply opening the hundreds of box prototypes, in order to understand and refine the customer's experience when receiving an Apple product.[74]

Figure 63: Apple are the masters of design simplicity

Key points in Chapter 6

- Effective print marketing depends on sending a message that's easy to understand.
- Less is more in clear communications.
- Each message only needs to get the reader to the next stage, it doesn't need to include all the details of a product.
- You must identify your business and clarify the nature of your product.
- Show your audience how to take the next steps to buy your product or take other actions.
- Know what your overall goal is and how your print strategy serves this agenda.
- The artwork must answer the three questions
- Who?
- What?
- How?
- Artwork's information balance will change depending on whether it is for early contact and late contact.

References

1   Confessore, N., Dance, G., Harris, R. and Hansen, M., 2021. The Follower Factory (Published 2018). [online] Nytimes.com. Available at: <https://www.nytimes.com/interactive/2018/01/27/technology/social-media-bots.html>

2   thinkbox. 2021. TV Nation 2016: research charts. [online] Available at: <https://www.thinkbox.tv/research/nickable-charts/thinkbox-research-charts/tv-nation/>

3   Ebiquity. 2021. Re-evaluating media for recovery. [online] Available at: <https://www.ebiquity.com/news-insights/press/re-evaluating-media-for-recovery/>

4   Growth Manifesto. 2021. How Super Coffee went from $0 to $400m valuation in 5 years | Growth Manifesto. [online] Available at: <https://www.growthmanifesto.com/supercoffee>.

5   Mehta, N. and Chugan, P., 2014. Impact of Visual Merchandising on Consumer Behavior: A Study of Furniture Outlets. Universal Journal of Management, 2(6), pp.207-217.

6   Hefer, Y. and Cant, M., 2013. Visual Merchandising Displays Effect on Consumers: A Valuable Asset or An Unnecessary Burden for Apparel Retailers. International Business & Economics Research Journal (IBER), 12(10), p.1217. Yolandé Hefer, University of South Africa, 2013 [publisher]

7   Gudonavičienė, R. and Alijošienė, S., 2015. Visual Merchandising Impact on Impulse Buying Behaviour. [online] Available at: <https://sciencedirect.com>.

8   Ritson, M., 2021. Drop the D-word!. [online] Hall & Partners. Available at: <https://www.hallandpartners.com/drop-the-d-word-mark-ritson> [Accessed 6 August 2021].

9   Holmes, Chet, Michael Gerber, and Jay Conrad Levinson. 2014. The Ultimate Sales Machine. New York: Portfolio.

10   Eagleman, D. and Hull, R., 2015. A communicator's guide to the neuroscience of touch. Boston, Massachusetts: Sappi.

11   Breaking Through the Noise. 2015. PDF. Canada Post Corporation.

12   "Quality Of Engagement for Catalogues Stands Apart from Other Channels". 2013. Roy Morgan. http://www.roymorgan.com/findings/8020-catalogues-engagement-circulation-june-2019-201906210514.

13   Sellen, Abigail J, and Richard Harper. 2003. The Myth of The Paperless Office. Cambridge, Mass.: MIT.

14   Sam, Upton. 2019. Fast Facts: Catalogue Model. PDF. Burnley: Real Media Collective. https://www.therealmediacollective.com.au/wp-content/uploads/2019/05/Fastfacts_CatalogueModel.pdf.

15   Fast Facts: Telecommunication. 2019. PDF. Burnley: Real Media Collective. https://www.therealmediacollective.com.au/wp-content/uploads/2019/05/Fastfacts_Telecommunication-1.pdf.

16   Kiran, Vasanth & Majumdar, Mousumi & Kishore, Krishna. 2012. Innovation in In-Store Promotions: Effects on Consumer Purchase Decision. European Journal of Business and Management. 4.

17   Bashar, Abu & Ahmad, Irshad. (2012). VISUAL MERCHANDISING AND CONSUMER IMPULSE BUYING BEHAVIOR: AN EMPIRICAL STUDY OF DELHI & NCR. International Journal of Retail Management and Research (IJRMR). 2. 31-41.

18   The Private Life of Mail. 2015. Ebook. Royal Mail Group Ltd.

19   Heilman, Carrie & Nakamoto, Kent & Rao, Ambar. 2002. Pleasant Surprises: Consumer Response to Unexpected In-Store Coupons. Journal of Marketing Research - J MARKET RES-CHICAGO. 39. 242-252. 10.1509/jmkr.39.2.242.19081.

20   Eagleman, D. and Hull, R., 2015. A communicator's guide to the neuroscience of touch. Boston, Massachusetts: Sappi.

21   Williams, Lawrence & Bargh, John. (2008). Experiencing Physical Warmth Promotes Interpersonal Warmth. Science (New York, N.Y.). 322. 606-7. 10.1126/science.1162548.

22   Eagleman, D. and Hull, R., 2015. A communicator's guide to the neuroscience of touch. Boston, Massachusetts: Sappi.

23 A Bias for Action: The Neuroscience Behind the Response-Driving Power of Direct Mail. 2015. PDF. Canada Post Corporation.

24 Ernst, Marc O. 2007. "Learning To Integrate Arbitrary Signals from Vision and Touch". Journal Of Vision 7 (5): 7. doi:10.1167/7.5.7.

25 The Private Life of Mail. 2015. Ebook. Royal Mail Group Ltd.

26 U.S. Postal Service Office of Inspector General. 2013. "Enhancing Mail for Digital Natives". https://www.uspsoig.gov/sites/default/files/document-library-files/2015/rarc-wp-14-001_enhancing_mail_for_digital_natives_0.pdf.

27 Soudry, Y., C. Lemogne, D. Malinvaud, S.-M. Consoli, and P. Bonfils. 2011. "Olfactory System and Emotion: Common Substrates". European Annals of Otorhinolaryngology, Head and Neck Diseases 128 (1): 18-23. doi:10.1016/j.anorl.2010.09.007.

28 Wilson, Donald A., and Regina M. Sullivan. 2011. "Cortical Processing of Odor Objects". Neuron 72 (4): 506-519. doi:10.1016/j.neuron.2011.10.027.

29 A Bias for Action: The Neuroscience Behind the Response-Driving Power of Direct Mail. 2015. PDF. Canada Post Corporation.

30 "Air Aroma Catalogue". 2020. https://www.air-aroma.com.au/.

31 A Bias for Action: The Neuroscience Behind the Response-Driving Power of Direct Mail. 2015. PDF. Canada Post Corporation.

32 *William, Powers. 2006. Hamlet's Blackberry: A Practical Philosophy for Building a Good Life in The Digital Age. US: Harper Collins.*

33 Sellen, Abigail J, and Richard Harper. 2003. The Myth of The Paperless Office. Cambridge, Mass.: MIT.

34 Jabr, Ferris. 2013. "Why the Brain Prefers Paper". Scientific American 309 (5): 48-53. doi:10.1038/scientificamerican1113-48.

35 "Catalogues - Top Ten Reasons". 2013. Letterbox Distributors. https://www.letterboxdistributors.com.au/catalogues-top-ten-reasons/.

36 "Creating Connections That Matter: How Australians Want to Hear from Brands". 2013. Association for Data-driven Marketing and Advertising (ADMA). https://auspost.com.au/business/business-admin/research-case-studies/research-reports/multichannel-marketing/creating-connections-that-matter-how-australians-want-to-hear-from-brands.

37 U.S. Postal Service Office of Inspector General. 2013. "Enhancing Mail for Digital Natives". https://www.uspsoig.gov/sites/default/files/document-library-files/2015/rarc-wp-14-001_enhancing_mail_for_digital_natives_0.pdf.

38 Olenski, Steve. 2021. "Four Key Principles of Cross Channel Marketing". Forbes. https://www.forbes.com/sites/steveolenski/2016/05/12/four-key-principles-of-cross-channel-marketing/.

39 "Tuned In: The Brain's Response to Ad Sequencing". 2017. Uspsoig. Gov. https://www.uspsoig.gov/sites/default/files/document-library-files/2017/RARC-WP-17-004.pdf.

40 Connecting For Action. 2016. Ebook. Canada Post. https://www.canadapost-postescanada.ca/cpc/doc/en/business/partner/160043Q-smm-connectivity-wp-digital.pdf.

41 "Tuned In: The Brain's Response to Ad Sequencing". 2017. Uspsoig.Gov. https://www.uspsoig.gov/sites/default/files/document-lbrary-files/2017/RARC-WP-17-004.pdf.

42 "Creating Connections That Matter: How Australians Want to Hear from Brands". 2013. Association for Data-driven Marketing and Advertising (ADMA).

43 "Catalogues - Top Ten Reasons". 2013. Letterbox Distributors. https://www.letterboxdistributors.com.au/catalogues-top-ten-reasons/.

44 "Value Of Paper and Print Report". 2012. Direct Mail - Top Ten Reasons. Brandscience.

45 U.S. Postal Service Office of Inspector General. 2013. "Enhancing Mail for Digital Natives". https://www.uspsoig.gov/sites/default/files/document-library-files/2015/rarc-wp-14-001_enhancing_mail_for_digital_natives_0.pdf.

46 Chakravorti, Bhaskar, and Ravi Shankar Chaturvedi. 2017. "Digital Planet 2017: How Competitiveness and Trust in Digital Economies Vary Across the World". Tufts University, The Fletcher School. https://sites.tufts.edu/digitalplanet/files/2020/03/Digital_Planet_2017_FINAL.pdf. July 2017

47 The Private Life of Mail. 2015. Ebook. Royal Mail Group Ltd.

48 Powers, William. 2006. Hamlet's Blackberry: Why Paper Is Eternal. [Cambridge, Mass.]: Joan Shorenstein Center on the

Press, Politics, and Public Policy, John F. Kennedy School of Government, Harvard University.

49 "Value Of Paper and Print Report". 2012. Direct Mail - Top Ten Reasons. Brandscience.

50 Hill, Catey. 2018. "Amazon and Ebay Are Betting on This Old-School Strategy to Drum Up Holiday Sales". Marketwatch. https://www.marketwatch.com/story/amazon-and-ebay-are-betting-on-this-old-school-strategy-to-drum-up-holidays-sales-2018-11-15.

51 2019. Thinkwithgoogle.Com. https://www.thinkwithgoogle.com/consumer-insights/consumer-trends/ar-shopping-interest-statistics.

52 "Programmatic Mail". 2016. Royal Mail. https://www.royalmail.com/business/marketing/mail/programmatic-mail.

53 U.S. Postal Service Office of Inspector General. 2013. "Enhancing Mail for Digital Natives". https://www.uspsoig.gov/sites/default/files/document-library-files/2015/rarc-wp-14-001_enhancing_mail_for_digital_natives_0.pdf.

54 "JICMAIL Home". 2017. Jicmail.Org.Uk. https://www.jicmail.org.uk/.

55 Gutierrez, Ben Paul B. 2008. "IN-STORE MEDIA: HOW EFFECTIVE ARE THEY? EVIDENCE FROM THE PHILIPPINES". Phillipine Management Review 15: 65-82.

56 "The New Multi-Screen World: Understanding Cross Platform Behavior, Google Think,". 2012. Services.Google.Com. https://services.google.com/fh/files/misc/multiscreenworld_final.pdf.

57 "Three Proven Ways to Boost Your Acquisition Strategy". 2018. Royal Mail Corporation.

58 Olenski, Steve. 2021. "Four Key Principles of Cross Channel Marketing". Forbes. https://www.forbes.com/sites/steveolenski/2016/05/12/four-key-principles-of-cross-channel-marketing/.

59 The Private Life of Mail. 2015. Ebook. Royal Mail Group Ltd.

60 "Path To Purchase Study". 2019. Thinkwithgoogle.Com. https://www.thinkwithgoogle.com/consumer-insights/consumer-trends/purchase-decision-time-data/.

61 PricewaterhouseCoopers. 2015. "Total Retail 2015: Retailers and The Age of Disruption". PricewaterhouseCoopers. https://www.pwc.com/id/en/publications/assets/cips/total-retail-february-2015.pdf.

62 "Think With Google". 2019. Thinkwithgoogle.Com. https://www.thinkwithgoogle.com/consumer-insights/consumer-trends/store-visit-after-online-research-data/.

63 The Private Life of Mail. 2015. Ebook. Royal Mail Group Ltd.

64 "The Salvation Army IPA Effectiveness Award Entry, MC&C (Silver)". 2014.

65 *Warde, Beatrice, and Henry Jacob. 1956. The Crystal Goblet. Cleveland: The World Publishing Company.*

66 Gutierrez, Ben Paul B. 2008. "In-store Media: How Effective are They? Evidence form the Philippines". Philippine Management Review 15: 65-82.

67 Gutierrez, Ben Paul B. 2008. " In-store Media: How Effective are They? Evidence form the Philippines ". Philippine Management Review 15: 65-82.

68 U.S. Postal Service Office of Inspector General. 2013. "Enhancing Mail for Digital Natives". https://www.uspsoig.gov/sites/default/files/document-library-files/2015/rarc-wp-14-001_enhancing_mail_for_digital_natives_0.pdf.

69 Warde, Beatrice, and Henry Jacob. 1956. The Crystal Goblet. Cleveland: The World Publishing Company.

70 Bill, Valentine Tschebotarioff. 1987. Chekhov--The Silent Voice of Freedom. New York: Philosophical Library.

71 Mehta, Neha P., and Pawan Kumar Chugan. 2014. "Impact of Visual Merchandising on Consumer Behavior: A Study of Furniture Outlets". Universal Journal of Management 2 (6): 207-217. doi:10.13189/ujm.2014.020601.

72 The Private Life of Mail. 2015. Ebook. Royal Mail Group Ltd.

73 Lashinsky, Adam. 2012. Inside Apple. London: John Murray.

74 Eagleman, D. and Hull, R., 2015. A communicator's guide to the neuroscience of touch. Boston, Massachusetts: Sappi.

75 Lashinsky, Adam. 2012. Inside Apple. London: John Murray.

CPSIA information can be obtained
at www.ICGtesting.com
Printed in the USA
LVHW042349011122
732016LV00013B/588